CHILDREN, FAMILIES & CITIES

PROGRAMS THAT WORK AT THE LOCAL LEVEL

National League of Cities
John E. Kyle, Editor

December 1987

Funding for this project was provided by a grant from the Foundation for Child Development.

Copyright © 1987 by the
National League of Cities
Washington, D.C. 20004
ISBN 0-933-729-32-4

Price: $10.00 per copy to NLC members.
         $15.00 per copy to Non-members.
         Please add $2.00 for postage and handling.
         Special rates available for multiple copies.

Table of Contents

Preface

Cities are people. Our children are our future.

This book builds on these two thoughts and on the increasing concern among the elected leadership of the nation's cities that too many children and their families are in trouble and require attention *now*. *Children, Families & Cities* provides analyses of distinct, but interrelated, problems and profiles of local programs that address those problems. As the national association for all of America's municipalities, the National League of Cities is very pleased to offer this important book to elected municipal officials, state municipal leagues, and others who share these concerns about city children and their families.

Children, Families & Cities makes important connections between areas of social policy and the activities of city and town governments. We congratulate and commend the authors and especially John E. Kyle – who served as editor, author and director of the project – for their excellent work. We join them in acknowledging and thanking the many people who contributed to the success of this project, especially the local government officials and other program staff who provided information about the projects and activities described here.

We are especially grateful to the Foundation for Child Development which provided a grant to the National League of Cities Institute to make this study possible. The Foundation for Child Development is a private foundation that makes grants to educational and charitable institutions. Its main interests are advocacy and public information projects, service experiments in New York City, and research that helps translate theoretical knowledge about children at risk into policies and practices that affect their daily lives.

Publication of *Children, Families & Cities* reflects NLC's commitment to providing research, education, and other assistance to municipal officials who seek to serve better their cities' residents and to improve the art and science of local governance. This book will also be of interest to the broader policy and research communities and to program practitioners. We invite comments and discussion about this volume.

We look forward to working further on these issues with others who share our sense of urgency and significance about the children of our cities and the cities of our future.

Alan Beals
Executive Director

William E. Davis, III
Director, Office of Policy
Analysis and Development

Editor's Acknowledgments

I am indebted to many individuals who provided substantive ideas, technical assistance, and comfort. The book is the better for all of their contributions.

The other authors gave many ideas and many hours of work. Their chapters reflect notable contributions to the information base about what is happening in cities and towns concerning children and families. The authors join me in thanking the many individuals who generously shared information for the profiles.

Jane Dustan, representing the Foundation for Child Development, provided comments that were thoughtful and always helpful.

The NLC staff welcomed me and helped me in many ways. Special thanks are due to Bill Barnes, NLC's Director of Research, with whom I established easy rapport, and who made many meaningful suggestions.

Clint Page served as a tireless publisher and technical editor. His efforts have moved us toward a book that will be attractive to the eye and friendly to the reader.

Many city hall officials across the country lent their expertise. They suggested themes, recommended programs to profile, and encouraged us. Chief among them were those who critiqued the book's early outline, individual chapters, and/or the book as a whole. They are Janet Hively of Minneapolis, Donna James of Seattle, Thomas Otto of Indianapolis, Pamela Plumb of Portland, Maine, Jacquie Swaback of Sacramento, and Maria Ward of Southfield, Michigan.

Substantive reviews and suggestions were provided by knowledgeable people who worked with us cheerfully and professionally despite the press of time and commitments. They are: June Bucy of the National Network of Runaway and Youth Services, Madeleine Kimmich, Don Mathis of the National Youth Employment Coalition, Lisa Mihaly of the Children's Defense Fund, Gwen Morgan of Work/Family Directions, Michelle Seligson of the School-Age Child Care Project, Lawrence Schweinhart of the High/Scope Educational Research Foundation, Lucy Watkins of the Center for Law and Education, Judith Weitz of the Children's Defense Fund, and Barbara Willer of the National Association for the Education of Young Children.

Joan Cobb Wilson provided her usual graciousness, support, and wit.

John E. Kyle

Contributors

Sharon Adams-Taylor is the Coordinator of the Adolescent Pregnancy Prevention Clearinghouse at the Children's Defense Fund. She has worked extensively in policy and practice around issues of at-risk youth, young children, and families. She holds a M.P.H. in Maternal and Child Health from the University of North Carolina and has professional experience in both the health and education sectors.

Marcia I. Cohen is a writer and researcher who specializes in youth and juvenile justice issues and has written extensively about model youth programs. She has conducted research and program evaluations for the Department of Health and Human Services, National Institute of Justice, National Children's Advocacy Center, and the State of Virginia, as well as for other agencies. She recently wrote *Identifying and Combating Juvenile Prostitution: A Manual for Action* for the National Association of Counties. Ms. Cohen is a vice-president of Development Services Group, Inc., a Bethesda, Maryland consulting firm.

John E. Kyle, the NLC Project Director responsible for *Children, Families & Cities*, is an advocate and administrator with twenty years experience in state and local programs and policies concerning children, youth, and families. In Maryland, as Director of the Office for Children and Youth for former governor Harry R. Hughes, he led the development and passage of major gubernatorial initiatives and edited *Building for the Future: The Status of Children and Children's Programs in Maryland*. In Michigan, he was a Policy Associate for the High/Scope Educational Research Foundation, where he helped develop and implement the Voices for Children project. In Pennsylvania, he was the Project Director of the Turtle Creek Valley Day Care Project.

Mary Morich is the Administrative Associate in the Adolescent Pregnancy Prevention Clearinghouse at the Children's Defense Fund. She has been working on the issues of preventing adolescent pregnancy and building youth self-sufficiency among minority and disadvantaged youth. She holds a B.A. from Trinity College in Washington, D.C.

Carol A. Morrow provides consulting and fund development services through Non-Profit, an independent effort to obtain equipment, funds, and community support for organizations serving the disadvantaged. She earned a Master's Degree in Social Work from the University of Maryland School of Social Work and Community Planning.

Karen Johnson Pittman is the Director of the Adolescent Pregnancy Prevention Policy Divison at the Children's Defense Fund. A sociologist, she has written numerous books and articles on topics as varied as sex education, the inter-relationship between work and family life, and the effects of federal budget cuts on the needy. At the Children's Defense Fund she is the writer and editor of a series of reports on adolescent pregnancy prevention that broaden our under-standing and correlate the causes and consequences of early parenthood, par-ticularly among disadvantaged teens.

Marjorie K. Smith is an advocate for children and a consultant on children's is-sues. She has worked in the private and public sectors at the federal, state, and local levels, including fifteen years as board member, director of public policy, or president of the Maryland Committee for Children. She earned a Master's Degree in Public Administration from the Maxwell School at Syracuse Univer-sity.

The KidsPlace logo is the trademark of Seattle's commitment to making the city a place that welcomes children and their families. Used with permission.

Chapter I

Introduction
by John E. Kyle

> *"I sense a new awakening on the part of the people of the United States: a realization that we can't ignore pressing social problems."*
> Arthur J. Holland, Mayor, Trenton, N.J.

Today's children and their families are beleaguered by changing economic, social and educational forces that challenge their resolve and resources, and those of public officials:

- By 1995, three-quarters of all school-age children and two-thirds of all preschool children will have mothers in the labor force. (Phillips, *Quality in Child Care*)

- More than 20 percent of our children live in poverty.

- Mobility is the norm, and a close-knit, extended family is the exception.

- More than one child in five lives in a single-parent household.

- Report after report expresses concern that schools are not meeting the needs of their students at the same time that the job market is requiring better-trained workers.

- The Committee for Economic Development reports that dropout rates "typically range from 30 to 50 percent in predominantly poor, minority school districts....of those students who receive high school diplomas, perhaps half have reading and writing skills that are inadequate for the job market." (*Children in Need*)

Some of these forces, such as poverty and homelessness, are causing increasingly poor conditions in the lives of city residents and are therefore emerging as important issues for city leaders, according to the 1986 National League of Cities survey of elected officials. Because local officials are the closest, most accessible sources of help, efforts to address the needs of children and families are emerging in cities and towns all across America.

This book, developed with support from the Foundation for Child Development, profiles more than thirty such local programs and policies. The first of the six primary chapters looks at the policy and planning context in which child- and family-related issues are examined. It calls attention to the need for comprehensiveness and for coordination in order to implement programs and policies strategically:

- Strategic planning and program coordination

  "Children's needs cut across organizational boundaries. The system of child and family services must depend on both interdepartmental cooperation and the alliance of state government with community-based groups and organizations." (Michigan *Children's Agenda*)

The next four chapters deal with issue areas affecting children and their families:

- Child care

  "Six million children across America need child care, but only about one million licensed child care slots exist." (Family Focus)

- Youth employment

  The unemployment rate for high school dropouts is two to three times greater than for high school graduates.

Introduction

- Homelessness

  "...hundreds of thousands of children and parents will become homeless this year alone." (National Coalition for the Homeless)

- Adolescent pregnancy prevention

  "Each year more than one million American teens become pregnant — four out of five unintentionally." (Children's Defense Fund)

The concluding chapter of the book offers some lessons learned from this project about how best to serve children and families at the city and town level. These lessons provide a framework from which new or improved programs can be launched.

These issues aren't the only child- and family-related issues. However, each of these topics is significant in and of itself. Taken together they help to illuminate the complexity and interrelatedness of the entire field. This selection of topics permits exploration of ranges of interest: for example, prevention (as provided through greater availability of affordable housing and high-quality child care) vs. remediation (as provided through emergency shelters or educational retraining efforts). There is also the opportunity to examine the needs of a range of ages from the infants needing child care to the teen parents needing employment assistance. The range of numbers is another variable — from the millions of pre-school children needing child care to to the hundreds of thousands of homeless teenagers to the ten thousand pregnant teens under fourteen needing preparation for parenthood. And some of these topics, like child care and effective schooling, apply fairly evenly to all families with children; others, like homelessness, apply more acutely to a more limited number of families. This set of issues, then, is a reasonable selection of the issues facing children and families and deserves careful attention.

The profiles presented in this book are not the only examples of local efforts. Rather, they are a sampling of what is happening. They reflect a wide range in demographics, size, and geography; in methodology of approach; and in extent of local government involvement. Many have been suggested by program and city hall experts across the country. Others were noted in responses to an advertisement in *Nation's Cities Weekly*, NLC's weekly newspaper.

This book is designed to provide city officials and others across the country with practical descriptions of effective programs that have the potential for replication or adaptation in other locales. The goal is to stimulate implementation of programs and policies that will improve the lives of children and their families.

Each of the chapters in this book focuses on one topic. The discussion of the topic includes definitions, statistics, causes, effects, and general information. Together these items constitute the "background" section in each chapter. Following the background, each chapter focuses on analyzing major issues or themes pertinent to the topics. These analyses provide a framework of ideas and issues that need to be considered before implementing a project or policy. Each chapter also contains some concluding remarks and an introduction to the profiles that follow (including a table listing their salient features).

Following the issues analysis in each chapter is a section of five to eight profiles of local programs or policies. These profiles have been selected to exemplify the issues presented. Several different authors have prepared these chapters, and each has a different style. In addition to the differing styles, different topics and different local programs have varying amounts of information available. However, similar information is provided in each profile, and each profile is presented in a similar format. Each one includes information about the program's startup, its budget, any outcome data available, tips on adapting it in other localities, and the name, address, and telephone number of a program contact person.

There is a short list of references and selected resources at the end of each chapter. The text mentions source material informally; the references refer to them more completely.

City officials offer a variety of arguments to support the efforts described in the profiles.

- First and foremost, the needs of city residents must be met.

- Second, it is clear that the children of today are the leaders of tomorrow. As today's adults live longer, it is clear that today's children will influence the quality of life for themselves as well as for those preceding them. Therefore, it is in the best self-interest of communities as well as individuals to give children the best opportunities possible for positive growth and development.

- Third, an ever-enlarging body of evidence is proving that there is enormous value in human service programs—both to the recipient of service and to the surrounding community: e.g., good preschool programs reduce school failure and help develop employability; prenatal care reduces the amount of high-cost medical care and improves the ability to learn. According to the September 1987 report of the Committee for Economic Development,

4

"improving the prospects for disadvantaged children is not an expense but an excellent investment."

- Fourth, the city and town is where the people are, and where the service is delivered. Some important planning, policy, and funding decisions might be made many miles away in the state or national capital; nevertheless, it is the responsibility and the right of local officials and citizens to ensure that their children's needs and interests are met.

- Fifth, it is at the local level that one can most sensitively balance the need of encouraging individual family responsibility with the need of maintaining communities that are livable and economically viable. In the past many issues affecting children were the sole province of the family. However, the complexity of the problems affecting children today inevitably means that society as a whole is also affected: the costs of school failure or unemployment or too-early childbearing burden all of us.

- Sixth, cities need to be more livable in order to attract and retain the young families who can contribute to local economic development as jobholders and taxpayers. For example, an NLC survey of officials from small cities points out that the flight of young people from such cities is weakening city efforts to attract jobs and remain economically viable.

Responding to critics concerned about his city's increasing efforts on behalf of children and youth, Mayor Don Fraser of Minneapolis said in his State of the City report,

"If our citizens are in trouble, we must serve as advocates to secure responses from other levels of government, and as catalysts to mobilize the resources represented by citizen volunteers and corporate giving. As we plan for improved opportunities for our youth, we must look beyond the resources of the schools or the city to get the job done. And where we do draw on our own financial resources, we should do so with the understanding that careful investments in our youth now can avoid larger public costs later."

Analyzing the issues raised by these selected topics, examining the local programs that are profiled, and reviewing the lessons learned from those programs will help prepare a concerned parent, civic leader, educator, or local elected official to support programs and policies that improve the lives of children and families. As a city hall staff member in Sacramento, California said, "Cities that are going to be viable for the future will be comfortable for families. The cities that catch on first will be the leaders of the 21st century."

References

Children's Defense Fund. 1987. *A Children's Defense Budget*. Washington, DC.

Committee for Economic Development. 1987. *Children in Need: Investment Strategies for the Educationally Disadvantaged*. New York and Washington.

Congressional Budget Office. 1985. *Reducing Poverty Among Children*. Washington, D.C.: Congress of the United States.

Emig, C. 1986. *Caring for America's Children*. Chicago: Family Focus.

Michigan Coalition for Children and Families. 1987. "FY 1988 Children's Agenda." Lansing, MI.

National Coalition for the Homeless. *Safety Network*. May 1987.

National League of Cities. 1986. "1986 Elected Officials Survey: Summary of Results." Washington, D.C.

National League of Cities. 1987. *The State of the Small City. Washington, D.C...*

National League of Cities. 1987. *Poverty in America: New Data, New Perspectives*. Washington, D.C.

Phillips, D. (ed.). 1987. *Quality in Child Care*. Washington, D.C.: National Association for the Education of Young Children.

Chapter II

Strategic Planning and Program Coordination

by John E. Kyle

> *"'One who goes looking for ivory will find an elephant attached.' We may seek a system of child care policies, but we will...need to involve ourselves in the elephantine issues of food programs, AFDC legislation, tax laws, health care..."*
>
> *The Rev. Eileen Lindner,*
> *"Danger: Our National Policy of Child Carelessness"*

Although Rev. Lindner was speaking about child care policy, she may as well have been speaking about any issues affecting children and families. Educational policy, for instance, seems straightforward enough. But a child's success in school may depend on:

- health factors (sufficient nutrition; immunizations; early pre-natal care to the mother to avoid childhood disabilities);

- family income (sufficient funds for books and supplies and for necessities like warm clothes and shoes to attend school in winter);

- housing (sufficient space and light to study at night);

7

- parenting (how much education the parent has received; availablity of parents to provide help with home work);

- teacher quality (teacher training and satisfactory teacher salaries and working conditions); and

- school curriculum (appropriate to the needs of the child).

Addressing any one piece without considering the others may not do much good. A child's success in school will be the result of successful attention to a great many factors, only some of which are noted above.

So it is with any attempt to improve the lives of children and families. The Annie E. Casey Foundation and the Center for the Study of Social Policy stated in February 1987 that such efforts are

> "...plausible only if there is community-wide support and involvement. Teachers by themselves cannot be expected to initiate and sustain these changes, nor can superintendents, business leaders, or local government — not until all of them, together with parents, community organizations and even state government policy makers agree that improving the skill level [and life chances] of at-risk youth is a central community objective."

Cooperation, comprehensiveness, and coordination emerge as key elements in the effective delivery of services to children and families. It is important to recognize the impact one part of the service delivery system may have on another, and it is important to recognize the inter-relatedness of the various needs of children and their families.

It is also essential, however, to devote sufficient thought and energy to the development of strategic plans. Proposed actions need careful planning as well as a cooperative spirit. Careful planning emerges from sound information gathering and from thoughtful analysis of the material collected. It is important to gather information about the needs of the children and families, but it is also important to gather information about various approaches to meeting those needs. The analysis will not only try to determine what causes the needs, but will also determine what kinds of efforts to address them in this locale will be most effective. It is as important to reject some proposed solutions that will not work as it is to accept others that will.

Issues and Analysis

The first issue is **political will**. The late 1980s appear to be a time when political leaders can invest in children and families and can expect to receive public support. Recently, KidsPac, a political action committee that supports candidates committed to children's issues, commissioned a public opinion survey. In concluding that voters will support candidates who are so committed, KidsPac founder William Harris said, "We've known for a long time that putting money into children's programs is good economics and good science. [The poll results suggest that] it can be good politics." He also said, "Voters have a huge amount of common sense. Pretty soon it will become increasingly evident that the cost of doing nothing exceeds the cost of making intelligent investments in young families and young children."

Four out of the ten major city issues identified in the Election '88 project of the National League of Cities Institute directly affect children and families: education, poverty, drug abuse, and children at risk. Most of the major presidential candidates have offered opinions and some solutions on child- and family-related issues, some of which are presented as part of Election '88 materials.

Tom Smith of the University of Chicago's National Opinion Research Center reported in April 1987 that "People favor allowing local government to exercise more power and responsibility...since local governments are smaller and nearer they are potentially more responsive to the public will." Taken together, these various factors indicate that the public will and the plans of elected officials are converging on significant and useful investment in meeting the needs of children and families. And the following profiles demonstrate the practical application of these factors: Pinellas County, Minneapolis, and Seattle have had legislative and/or voter support for new child- and family-related initiatives.

A second issue is that **solving the dilemma of prevention vs. cure needs to be a major part of the planning equation**. Too often, as Therese Lansburgh has noted, "We have waited until the child is damaged, or the family broken, before we try to help. We are closing the barn door, in effect, after the horse has run away."

In the past, lack of attention to prevention might be rationalized because a lack of conclusive evidence supported it. Now, however, many research studies show the value of investment in children. For example, the Centers for Disease Control reports that every dollar spent to immunize children against measles saves more than $7 in reduced illness and hospitalization costs; yet many children are not immunized. The High/Scope Educational Research Foundation reports that

9

high quality early childhood education can help prevent school failure, and can return $6 for every dollar invested in a one-year program for poor children, based primarily on savings from reduced special education enrollment and on estimates of future savings from higher levels of employment, less reliance on public assistance, and fewer arrests. However, less than half of the poor children eligible, according to educational need, have high-quality early childhood education available to them.

It is important to provide resources for remediation and rehabilitation, but it may be even more important to provide resources to prevent the need for them. William Milliken, former governor of Michigan, chairs the selection committee of Harvard University's Innovations in State and Local Governments Awards program. In presenting a positive picture of local government's capacity to respond imaginatively to pressing social and economic needs and to demonstrate valuable lessons learned, Milliken notes, "One such lesson is the value of relatively inexpensive preventive programs rather than costly after-the-fact remedial projects." Pinellas County programs have focused on those with prevention themes, and such themes are strongly encouraged in Pittsburgh.

The third issue is **the importance of the neighborhood**. City Councilman John Maloney of Columbus, Ohio suggests that "A guiding principle that might ease the coordination between multiple levels of government as well as private agencies and more fully exploit local resources could be the acceptance of a standardized, defined community on a scale similar to a high school district." Then, Maloney adds, community programs can fit "the scale of an individual's time, distance, and neighborhood orientation."

Cities in Schools (CIS) is an example of an organization that focuses on neighborhoods by focusing on local schools. Founded in 1976, CIS now operates in twenty-three cities, establishing coordinated service teams to deliver educational and social services to students in schools with high dropout rates. Local schools are the focal point because they are centrally located and easily accessible in most neighborhoods.

The concept of multi-service or "one stop shopping" centers to assist families is being used in Baltimore through community- and church-based Family Support Centers and in Minneapolis through the Public Housing Authority's Family Learning Center. The principles that guide establishment of such programs include ease of accessibility to clients, comprehensiveness of services, and readiness of clients to use the facility.

Careful data collection and analysis is the fourth issue. It is important to have facts, but it is more important to have credible facts and even more important to integrate them well into strategic planning and policy development. Community sources of data include the school system, churches, media, voluntary organizations, social service and health departments, the district attorney, the United Way, and public officials. Each has a piece, and their sum can provide a clearer overall picture. It is important to make use of as many sources as possible because data collection is not consistent. One program may collect some items; another may collect others. The planning decision, however, may depend on items from both sources. Program administrators must be wary of these holes in the data collection system and work to close them. It is important to keep careful track of sources, cross check references, and maintain a single-point-in-time approach (so that figures from different years are not inappropriately compared for instance).

The New Futures initiative of the Annie E. Casey Foundation, designed to assist selected cities in meeting the needs of at-risk youth, provides some useful insights regarding data collection and analysis. It is important to collect "problem measures" (number of teen births, number of dropouts, etc.), but it is also important to determine where and how these overlap (e.g. how many teen parents are also dropouts, how much of the demand for child care is from teen parents). The degree of overlap is what will challenge planners and strategists to be coordinative and comprehensive in their approaches. It is also important to determine the demographics behind the numbers (e.g. the race and gender of the dropouts, the neighborhoods in which they live). Surveys in Sacramento and Seattle have contributed data to the planning process and have stimulated solutions that cut across various city agencies and served various populations.

Collecting this information is just one step, however. The community must next choose **how it looks at the problem** – the fifth issue. Will it use an approach that "explains" the problems based on low-socioeconomic status, based on the consequence of community policies and practices, or based on the attitudes, values and characteristics of the youth themselves and/or their families? No one of these is the complete answer. The additional focus needed is on the changes youth-serving institutions themselves may need to make in their operations. Their policies or practices may be causing or exacerbating the very problems they are trying to ameliorate. Information is needed on these youth-serving agencies: not just a list of them, but an analysis of who and how many they serve, where and how, and with what success. Looking both at the problem presented and at the

11

potential problem solver should lead to the best solution. For instance, Seattle encourages child care but also monitors the providers.

A sixth issue is **whether effective planning and coordination require postponing urgent or feasible action.** A preferred answer is "No, but...." No—immediate specific actions ought not to be put off while voluminous reports are prepared. But—as much as possible, strategic questions should be asked and answered even as a project is initiated. Planning and coordination are not something above and separate from project implementation; they are a part of it. Minneapolis is preparing a twenty-year plan to meet the needs of its children and families. However, specific programs are being put in place during the interim. As these individual elements are needed, they are implemented. They contribute to the overall plan, but they are not totally dependent on it.

Profiles

Communities are using many different ways to achieve comprehensive planning and program coordination concerning children and families.

In Seattle, Washington, service groups, individuals, and mayoral leadership have created KidsPlace, which has used creative city boosterism and concrete child- and family-oriented programs to attract families to the city.

In Minneapolis, Minnesota, representatives of all the local elected bodies constitute the legislatively-created Youth Coordinating Board in order to cut across all services being delivered to children and families and create a continuum of services from birth to age twenty.

A geographically-focused charitable foundation in Pittsburgh, Pennsylvania, has used city leaders and experts from all walks of life to examine the hallmarks of the city's past forty years in order to plan comprehensively for the next forty years.

A routine feasibility study in Sacramento, California, led to a comprehensive survey of children and parents that is influencing the way the city treats its families.

Pinellas County, Florida, has a dedicated funding mechanism that provides local tax dollars to add to the planning and service base for the county's children and families.

Resources and references follow the profiles on page 34.

KidsPlace: A Kids' Lobby for a Vital Seattle
Seattle, Washington

Attracting and retaining families as city residents with comprehensive initiatives benefiting children.

Contact:
Donna James
Office of the Mayor
1200 Municipal Building
Seattle, WA 98104
206/684-4000

The KidsPlace project in Seattle, Washington is one of the better known examples of a comprehensive response to the needs of a city's children and families. It uses ingenious public relations, creative programming and solid city-administration initiatives.

KidsPlace received its initial impetus from individuals and organizations outside city government. Ultimately, however, KidsPlace was jointly founded by the city (which wanted to strengthen its reputation as a family town), the Junior League (which had a tradition of serving children), and the YMCA (which had an extensive repertoire of services for kids and few kids to use them). The project moved ahead with the wholehearted endorsement of Seattle Mayor Charles Royer and with funding from the sponsors and from local businesses and foundations.

The program was developed partly in response to 1980 U.S. Census figures documenting the city's rapidly declining population of children and youth during the 1970s. The overall population dropped 7 percent, but the children and youth population dropped 36 percent. Seattle had had a reputation as a family town, a good place in which to raise kids. But during the late 1960s and 1970s, Seattle's political and cultural climate favored young professionals and the elderly more than families with children. Seattle, like most American cities, became more and more designed for adult use. But Seattle also has a reputation as a city that can be what it wants to be, rather than a city that passively adapts to demographic and economic trends perceived to be beyond its control. KidsPlace aims to place children and their families high on Seattle's political, economic and cultural agenda. It aims to attract more families with children and to support and keep those families with children already living in Seattle.

Among the first steps taken was a 1984 survey of Seattle's children and youth to determine what they thought Seattle would look like if it were to be a good and healthy place for kids. What things needed to be changed? How did the children describe commonly known elements of the city? What was the dirtiest place in town? What was the most fun place to go? The 6,700 survey responses have helped city officials determine, for example, that steps were needed around some of the aquarium's exhibits so smaller children could see them, that teenagers could make use of roving Community Service Officers who could provide information such as where to go for shelter, and that the Seattle Parks Department could take a closer look at the design of parks and play equipment. Mayoral aide Donna James says, "We don't see KidsPlace as a project, but as an attitude. When people make policies, we want them to start thinking in terms of how the policy will affect children and families."

The results of the 1984 survey and related input on children and family issues resulted in a planning document, *The KidsPlace Action Agenda 1985-1990*, subtitled "Looking at the city with children in mind." More than 300 volunteers serving on six task forces developed thirty goals aimed at making Seattle a better place for children and families. Work toward some of these goals — among them creating a kids bike route network, fighting adult exploitation of children, expanding playground and park programs, marketing the public schools, reducing bus fares for children and youth, and expanding multi-cultural opportunities for kids — is under way. The thirty items, prioritized from an original list of 600, are included because they are "do-able" and achievable within five years. The plan not only describes the action needed but also describes where the responsibility for action lies.

The survey has also provided impetus for other items. A KidsBoard of forty teenagers lobbies city hall on issues that run the gamut from fighting against a city-proposed midnight curfew on teenagers to supporting competency tests for local school teachers. An annual KidsDay promotes positive activities for children by providing free museum admissions, free bus rides, and other incentives. On KidsDay, all KidsPlaces — from the zoo to the elevator at the Space Needle — are free to children sixteen and under.

KidFriendly Downtown is a new program that has been recently added to the KidsPlace repertoire. City officials would like downtown Seattle to be viewed as friendly to children. They began a campaign to enlist store owners and shop keepers who would welcome children on their premises. Stores with the Kid-Friendly logo in their windows are the ones where children can feel free to go and seek assistance. "I ran out of money; I need to call my mom and make sure I get a ride home" or "I need to use the bathroom". These are simple things that help to achieve KidsPlace's major goal of fostering a place and an atmosphere in which families would want to live rather than leave. They would like to stay because it is child friendly—a place where children and families are made to feel welcome.

In addition to these efforts that serve to publicly announce that Seattle welcomes children and families, the mayor has taken several significant administrative steps. Under the Royer administration, the city budget process requires that every department from the health department to the water department suggest children's initiatives in their annual budget submissions. Some departments may not always have an initiative, but each department is asked in order to emphasize the Mayor's overall concern for children and families. The initiatives submitted by the departments make up a set of proposed children's initiatives, from which the mayor chooses those that augment a coordinated plan for services to children and families. An annual report on the status of Seattle's children is released as part of the KidsDay celebration.

Seattle's mayor is providing the leadership to characterize the city as a "KidsPlace". Efforts are under way, however, to institutionalize some elements of the KidsPlace philosophy and attitude. Zoning requirements have been changed so that family day care is recognized as an allowable use for dwellings in the city and so that child care centers can operate on the second floor of buildings. Because of a KidsPlace recommendation, the mayor and city council have formed a commission on children and youth to help formulate a citywide youth policy.

KidsPlace itself is being more formally institutionalized. In the past it has been coordinated by an aide to the mayor; it has now been incorporated as a separate nonprofit entity so that there will be a continuing KidsPlace organization regardless of who is mayor. The KidsPlace concept will have a history and tradition and, at the same time, can continue to operate without being subjected to the whim of a future mayor with less commitment to children and families. Royer expects KidsPlace to endure because it is building a constituency among parents and politicians. City Councilman Jim Street says, "Programs with an emphasis on kids have received attention they might not have received otherwise. And I think even the symbolism is worth something, as a message."

Another form of institutionalization is taking place in the replication of KidsPlace concepts in other cities, including San Francisco, San Diego, San Antonio, and St. Louis. Royer's aide Donna James is encouraging them, but she also cautions them to take their own unique qualities into account — blind copy-catting will not work. Pediatrician Robert Aldrich, one of the guiding forces behind creation of Seattle's KidsPlace notes that replication may be easier in smaller cities, but that "supercities" could follow suit by approaching the project neighborhood by neighborhood. Focusing on the imperative to have KidsPlace, Aldrich adds, "Cities that are not favorable places for children to live in become places that adults don't want to live in, either."

KidsPlace is successful already, and it aims to improve on its success. One of the survey responses indicated that the city's parks were its most popular asset. Shortly thereafter, city voters passed a bond issue to renovate them; it appears that the survey results had a significant impact on passage. Businesses are expected to profit from increased activity when downtown shopping areas are made more attractive to families. A more important incentive is the fact that productive lives may be salvaged if the city can become a positive environment. Mayor Royer is pushing to ease some of the social problems affecting children by providing child care, youth employment programs, emergency youth shelters, and services to abused children. He says, "We're trying to look at everything we do in the city as it affects the health of children. Respect for kids is a basic equity we're trying to build into the city."

The KidsPlace replication in St. Louis, Missouri, has had two recent significant events. First, more than 300 residents including 25 youths participated in a day-long conference. They finalized a community plan and action agenda. Conference attendees included educators, government officials, mall management, developers, and representatives of youth-serving agencies. Therefore, prospects for implementation are high. Second, promotion of the concept got a boost this summer when a St. Louis television station produced and aired a special on children's needs. The sound track, made up primarily of voices of St. Louis youths, was played over footage showing the places youths go. The special has been broadcast twice and is available on loan. These two events follow the July 1987 publication of the results of a comprehensive survey of St. Louis area young people in the third through twelfth grades. For further information, contact Blair Forlaw, Executive Director, KidsPlace:St. Louis, 7736 Forsythe Boulevard, St. Louis, MO 63105; 314/727-5200.

Youth Coordinating Board
Minneapolis, Minnesota

Continuum of service from birth to age twenty.

Contact:
Richard Mammen, Executive Director
Youth Coordinating Board
Room 202
City Hall
Minneapolis, MN 55415
612/348-6995

Janet M. Hively
Deputy to the Mayor
City Hall
Minneapolis, MN 55415
612/ 348-2100

In its approach to the problems of children and families, Minneapolis focuses simultaneously on comprehensiveness (by striving to implement a comprehensive set of services for youths from the time they are born to the age of twenty) and instituting a process to guarantee continuing efforts on behalf of youth.

In the 1986 State of the City report, Mayor Don Fraser said that "the city is more than objects and buildings: it is people. Our children are those who in a few short years will be our adult neighbors, our workers, managers, consumers, and voters." Sporadic federal cutbacks in services to children and families are one impetus for Fraser's concern. He does not believe that it is necessarily the city's responsibility to replace lost state and federal funding, but he does view it as a city necessity to assemble the public and private resources to develop comprehensive human development programs.

The innovative "assembly" mechanism used in Minneapolis is the Youth Coordinating Board, which was created in 1986 by a joint powers agreement resulting from a 1985 state law authorizing such an agreement. The Board is a successor to an earlier organization created by the Mayor as a more informal task force in 1984. The agreement establishing the Board will last for five years.

The eleven-member Youth Coordinating Board is composed of representatives of each of the elected bodies in Minneapolis: the Mayor, city council, county commissioners, board of education, park board, library board, juvenile court judge, and the state senate and house delegations from the Minneapolis area. Each of these elected officials is responsible to the voters. Each has responsibilities for children and youth, some more narrowly focused than others. According to the joint powers agreement, the Youth Coordinating Board's purpose is "to improve the ability of public agencies and services to promote the health, safety, education, and development of the community's youth and to create an organizational structure to improve coordination among the agencies and services." In part, the charge requires them to blur some of the distinctions between them so that they can help each other meet the needs of youth.

The agreement establishing the Board also determined the initial budget of $100,000. The city, the county and the school district each provided $30,000; the Library Board provided $3,000, and the Park Board $7,000. A supplementary budget, which could include gifts and grants, can be established as determined by the Board.

The Youth Coordinating Board and the Mayor look at the first twenty years of life as a period over which a continuum of services is needed to meet the changing needs of children as they grow up. Fraser's 1986 report continues, "The purpose is to be able to demonstrate a measurable change through the twenty years which it takes for a new generation to grow up." The comprehensive set of services provides a skeleton of what ought to exist; an audit of what actually exists shows where work is needed to put flesh on the skeleton. The effort to establish and flesh out the services involves the entire community: the schools, neighborhoods, churches, voluntary organizations, social service agencies, and businesses.

The services cover the twenty years of youth in several stages. Infants and their mothers need maternal and child health care. Local dollars are used to support maternal and child health care, while Community Development Block Grant funds support a consortium of community clinics which serve low-income residents, and school-based clinics have been expanded. "Way to Grow" is an emerging plan to promote school readiness by providing services to help all parents with their children ranging from so-called "low-risk children" to "high-risk children."

When a child has reached the age of five, the emphasis has shifted to early childhood and parenting education and child care. The Mayor's office is providing advocacy support for proposed innovations (many of which were contributed by mayoral staff, e.g. identification of high-risk newborns through city hospitals) and for increased funding both from local school district authorities and from state and federal legislators.

By the time a child is twelve, educational support, youth volunteerism, recreation, and adolescent pregnancy prevention and parenting efforts are being emphasized. To provide opportunities for youth volunteerism, the Mayor's office, the Minneapolis Schools, and the Pillsbury Company created the "Fresh Force" program, which invites seventh and eighth graders to volunteer for community service. The Mayor's office houses and provides in-kind services for the Minneapolis Adolescent Pregnancy and Parenting Project, which was developed by community and youth agency leaders and funded by the McKnight Foundation. The project has two aims: preventing teen pregnancies and supporting teen parents and their children. Activities have included the publication of a *Directory of Services Addressing Adolescent Pregnancy and Parenting in the City of Minneapolis*, expansion of school-based health clinics, development of child care for teen parents in or adjacent to high schools, a series of speakouts, plays and media events focusing on pregnancy prevention, and curricula helping parents to talk with their children about human sexuality.

In the years leading up to eighteen, employability is the focus. City-supported efforts include a work internship program focused on potential school dropouts, a summer day labor program in city parks for youth at risk for involvement in gangs or other negative behavior, and a career beginnings program with activities such as one-on-one mentoring and assistance with college applications. As a youth moves into adulthood, the services deal with employment, housing, food, and welfare reform. One city activity is the Transitional Work-Internship Program, which find jobs in city departments for high school graduates who are having difficulty in securing employment a year after graduation. Supervision, counseling, and help in obtaining private sector jobs are provided during this period, which may last up to year.

The goal is to address these areas in tandem with each other rather than in isolation and to keep filling in the gaps between services until all the needs are met. "City's Children 2007," a twenty-year plan currently in the works, will chart where the Board and the city are going to be two years, five years, ten years, and twenty years from now in their efforts to build and implement the continuum of services.

Two other efforts are related to Minneapolis' overall effort. First, the Minneapolis Community Business Employment Alliance (MCBEA), a group of business leaders in the city, was formed by the Mayor in 1983. MCBEA is housed in the Chamber of Commerce; its activities include the publication in 1985 of one of the nation's more interesting early childhood education reports. Minneapolis business leaders are interested in early childhood education; they see high quality early childhood education as one of the best ways to improve the employability of adults. *Preventing Unemployment: A Case for Early Childhood Education* states, "By starting employability training in the early years Minneapolis has the opportunity to be a national leader — to provide business with a well-trained and educated labor force, to reduce government costs of long-term unemployment and to enrich the lives of children." MCBEA's most recent publication is *Building the Work Force: Developing Youth Employability*. This report points out that youths need basic skills, work experience, mentoring from caring adults, and a commitment for jobs and program funding from the business community. To implement both reports, MCBEA is developing the Minneapolis Youth Trust by asking local companies to provide money, employee time for mentoring, and jobs (for transitional work experience).

A second related effort is the creation of a comprehensive learning center in a rehabilitated building in a large family housing project administered by the Public Housing Authority. In this Family Learning Center, several agencies offer a variety of services related to family and child development. The services include early childhood and family education, adult basic education, English as a second language, job counseling, prenatal health care, and dental care. The concept and budget development came from the mayor's office, but implementation is being carried out by the Minneapolis schools and the Public Housing Authority.

These efforts show that Mayor Fraser "has concentrated on basic needs for housing, health care, nutrition and education for disadvantaged residents along the continuum of human development from birth to adulthood." This January 1987 overview of Fraser's effort continues by pointing out that he is seeking "to prevent dependency at later points in the developmental continuum by strengthening support early in life for later self-sufficiency."

The Pittsburgh Foundation and
The Howard Heinz Endowment
Pittsburgh, Pennsylvania

Charitable giving as a model of planning to meet the needs of a
city's children and families.

Contact:
Margaret M. Petruska, Program Officer
The Howard Heinz Endowment and
The Pittsburgh Foundation
Suite 1417
301 Fifth Avenue
Pittsburgh, PA 15222-2494
412/ 391-5122

Charitable giving is providing two models of leadership in program planning and
policy development to assist the children and families of Pittsburgh and western
Pennsylvania. One model is The Pittsburgh Foundation's innovative birthday
celebration that focused on its achievements during the previous forty years in
eight funding areas and the needs for the next forty years. The other, the Howard
Heinz Endowment, shows how a larger benefit or impact can be obtained by a
concerted analysis of giving. Both show promise as resources to city officials seeking creative partnerships to meet the needs of children and families.

The Pittsburgh Foundation is a community foundation. Its assets are amassed by
pooling restricted and unrestricted charitable funds in varying amounts from
people in all walks of life who can't necessarily establish their own foundation but
whose smaller amounts of money will benefit the common good when administered jointly with the gifts of others. In general, community foundations have
a very specific geographic focus. Depending on the size of their assets, the fact
that they are made up of lots of smaller and/or more restricted funds may make
it difficult for them to put together major efforts. Their very specific focus,
however, may make them the first to respond to critical community concerns.
(There are about 300 community foundations across the country. The Council on

Foundations, the *Foundation Directory*, or a library can provide information on where they are located.)

In 1986, The Pittsburgh Foundation, one of the ten largest community foundations in the country, convened committees composed of leaders from across the city, both in government and in the private sector, to participate in a unique celebration of the foundation's fortieth birthday. These leaders were asked to select five significant events or forces during the previous forty years that affected each of the foundation's eight primary giving areas. (One of these areas is children and youth; others, like health and education, are also important to the lives of children and families. These kinds of giving areas are typical of community foundations.) After the forty significant events were announced, the committees were reconvened to discuss the future. Forty-eight initiatives were identified that needed to be undertaken. The foundation itself added two that transcended the eight areas and could benefit all the initiatives, making an even fifty. In addition, the foundation committed itself to raising an additional fifty million dollars in endowment funds to meet the challenge of these fifty initiatives.

The Committee on Children and Youth noted many changes in American — and Pittsburgh — life. "Single-parent families, unemployed parents, poverty, widespread use of drugs and alcohol, and powerful media messages all contribute to the problems facing today's children." Six initiatives emerged from the committee's work:

- expanding services for at-risk and delinquent youth;
- coordinating services for children and families;
- curbing child abuse and neglect;
- increasing daycare services;
- focusing media attention on teen problems; and
- coordinating mental health services for children.

With creativity, a community foundation has mounted a significant portrait of Pittsburgh achievements and needs in its eight program areas. As a result, the generosity of many individuals will benefit the Pittsburgh community as a whole. The Pittsburgh Foundation itself is striving to alleviate the needs, but its portrait provides incentives for others — a base upon which others can help attend to the needs of Pittsburgh's children and families.

There are also foundations that are geographically focused but have been established in a more traditional way—through the largesse of one person rather than through the contributions of many. Pittsburgh's Howard Heinz Endowment, a private foundation, is one of those. Over a number of years, the Endowment supported many programs concerned with families and children. However, as Endowment trustees and staff examined what they were doing for children and youth, they realized that they had been giving sums of money to a large number of agencies, efforts, and projects without as much focus or aim as they wanted.

Thus, in 1985, the Endowment developed initiatives that have a greater focus in order to achieve maximum impact on an issue. Three foci became clear. The first is support of early intervention programs for children and families. To receive funds from the Endowment, the provider must serve an at-risk population, must include the child and the family, must serve the very young child, and must deliver a preventive service. Services in the neighborhood must be linked with each other. "Services are far too fragmented", says Program Officer Margaret Petruska. She encourages programs that are "comprehensive and integrating." They should make sure that all the child and family needs are being met across the continuum of existing services and all the elements of that continuum should be aware of, and use, each other's abilities. Other Pittsburgh organizations, like the United Way, are now moving toward this kind of collaboration, too. A new partnership emerged in this arena in 1986 when the Endowment and the U.S. Department of Health and Human Services jointly issued a request for proposals "which would identify very young children from low-income neighborhoods for whom early intervention would be beneficial." A three-year project has been funded called 'Families Facing the Future.' It targets eighty children in three Pittsburgh neighborhoods. Features include a home visitor resource for each family, a screening and assessment checklist for determining at-risk children, and a multi-agency approach that links thirty separate agencies to provide the tailored services necessary.

The second focus is to build upon and strengthen the Pittsburgh region's expertise in education, research, and training related to early childhood development. The establishment of the Office of Child Development at the University of Pittsburgh as a center of excellence is one illustration of this commitment. The goal for this Office is to help provide well-trained people to agencies and provide expert resources and research across the community. It too has an integrated approach. More than 150 university faculty members concerned with children, including social work, child development, education, sociology, and psychology, are being encouraged to promote interdisciplinary research and training. A center of excellence at the university should have staying power in support of agency efforts for children and families beyond what a grant to an agency can achieve.

A third focus is on government. The Endowment has been one of the motivators behind the establishment of the Allegheny County Commission on Children and Youth. (Allegheny County surrounds Pittsburgh.) The Commission, an example of the idea of a foundation using its prestige to convene groups to spearhead ideas, is intended to ensure that government is able to look at these issues and have access to ideas and trends. The Endowment is also supporting the re-organization efforts of the Allegheny County department of children and youth services. These efforts are aimed at institutionalizing new ideas and new commitment concerning children, youth, and families.

These charitable efforts reflect a mission of collaboration and of integrated service delivery. Petruska says, "If you strengthen the whole family, you strengthen the child...parents are their children's first teachers and their best teachers." She believes that city and foundation leaders share similar roles very well (convene, broker, leverage, crate new partnerships). In these roles they can be quite complementary in their support for children and families (the foundation can take risks with planning, evaluation or innovations; the city can provide ongoing operation).

A foundation's strength is its independence and its knowledge of a community, its agencies and its leaders without being a vested party. The downside of foundation involvement is its lack of staying power. The nature of a foundation is that it cannot be there for the long haul, although one year grants are now rare and three to five years of support is becoming customary.

Not only are children and families a focus of these Pittsburgh-based foundations, but they are also the focus of an emerging national affinity group for members of the Council on Foundations. The Grantmakers for Children and Youth have held two national conferences for their members, and their numbers are growing. Their efforts at learning and coordination are clear signs that foundation leadership can be a key element in the sophisticated world of strategic planning and program coordination related to child- and family-related policymaking.

Two reports supported by foundation grants are designed to have similar impact on the lives of children and families in other cities. In Baltimore, Maryland, the Morris Goldseker Foundation supported Peter Szanton's report, *Baltimore 2000*, which looks at the city's future without any intervention, charts a preferable future, and discusses how to achieve it. This controversial report has contributed to the debate in a mayoral election and has generated another report in response,

Destiny 2000, from the Baltimore Urban League. (For further information, contact Timothy D. Armbruster, Executive Director, Morris Goldseker Foundation of Maryland, 300 N. Charles Street, Baltimore, MD 21201; 301/837-5100.) In Illinois, the Colman Fund for the Well-Being of Children and Youth and other foundations convened a task force to develop *The Plan of Action for Children*. Its pivotal conclusions and eighty-one distinct recommendations are intended to be useful to Illinois planners and policymakers; however, they are also instructive to planners and policymakers outside Illinois. (For further information, contact the Colman Fund for the Well-Being of Children and Youth, c/o the Chicago Community Trust, 208 South LaSalle Street, Suite 850, Chicago, IL 60604.)

Planning Sacramento: Views of Students and Parents
Sacramento, California

Survey of students leading to positive impact on child care.

Contact:
Jacquie Swaback, Child Care Coordinator
Department of Parks and Community Services
City of Sacramento
1231 I Street
Suite 400
Sacramento, CA 95814-2977
916/449-5858

What if kids planned Sacramento? That question motivated the formation of the Urban Planning for Children Project Task Force as part of the Sacramento Child Care Coalition. The Task Force report has led to multi-faceted city programs, primarily related to child care activities.

The Task Force surveyed students (and some parents) in three major school districts in Sacramento, asking them how they would plan the area in terms of activities, transportation, commercial area design, housing and neighborhood design, child care, and "good places for kids in Sacramento." With a $50,000 budget, most of it gained from large numbers of $50 contributions and a few $5,000 contributions, a survey, similar to the one in Seattle, was devised by representatives from the private, public and academic sectors and administered in 1984-1985. The results were analyzed by California State University.

The concept for the Sacramento survey emerged from a feasibility study concerned with restoring an historic part of Sacramento that had formerly been a little town. What could happen in this particular part of Sacramento that would be advantageous for the future? The planners discovered that the presence of older people living in the neighborhood made it necessary to examine the needs of pedestrians. As the planners discussed the places that one could walk to, they realized that the other big population of pedestrians was children, especially those under sixteen who can't yet drive.

This interest in the needs of children led the planners to survey three major school district in Sacramento: one largely rural, one largely the urban core of Sacramento, and one largely suburban.

The results of the survey were published in *Planning Sacramento: Views of Students and Parents*. The book, subtitled "A Tourist's Guide for Today and a Developer's Guide for Tomorrow," covers the ways in which survey results are being implemented. It includes children's pictures, descriptions of good places for kids in Sacramento (complete with maps and bus routes) and a directory of Sacramento businesses especially supportive of children. (Copies of the book are available for five dollars each from the contact person noted above.)

From the beginning, the project was structured to implement the survey results. The project had four parts: assess what needs to be done, assess who has the resources to do it, structure the innovation to be in the self-interest of those with the resources, and support those who are implementing projects.

What did the survey bring to light? Kids and parents wanted more bus service, bike lanes, and sidewalks — so kids can get to places without a car. Kids would like to have more community swimming pools and places to dance. Kids would design commercial areas to include benches and drinking fountains for very short people. They would include child care centers and supervised play areas in shopping centers, so kids wouldn't have to always go shopping with their parents. Kids would build houses in which their bedrooms were big enough to include desks.

These results have been used primarily in planning and zoning hearings to present the views and desires of children and parents. In addition, there is a "Children and Youth Facilities" Section in Sacramento's *Central Business District Urban Design Plan* that addresses child care in the downtown area; the *North Natomas Community Plan* and the *General Plan Update* address putting child care facilities in residential, office/commercial/industrial, and school settings. The city planning staff has written *A Developer Checklist for Child Care Facilities* to guide developers.

A Child Care Task Force formed by Mayor Anne Rudin in 1985 brought together representatives from the public, private, schools, and parks sectors of Sacramento. One of its major recommendation was that the city hire a Child Care Coordinator; the part-time position, in the Parks and Community Services Department, was filled in January 1987 at an annual cost of approximately $20,000. The creation of a five-year plan under the guidance of a full-time coordinator with a full-time staff is under study.

Children, Families & Cities

The Child Care Coordinator has concentrated on four areas. One is the refinement of the process for approving child care facilities. Family day care homes for twelve or fewer children are now permitted by right in all residential zones. A future step is the development of a "one stop packet" for developers and providers who want to establish or expand child care centers. It will contain all needed forms for state licensing and local zoning and building permits, as well as a description of available resources.

A second direction has been the inclusion of child care benefits in the city's flexible benefit package for its employees. This not only benefits city employees, but also provides a model for other employers.

A third city effort is aimed at raising the salaries of child care providers. The city recently hired a number of people to provide before- and after-school child care at thirteen school district sites. Their jobs were compared with existing city jobs requiring similar education, responsibility, and experience rather than with the child care market. As a result, the salaries are higher than market rate, and all the fringe benefits of being a city employee are included. The city is now working with private child care providers to improve private salaries.

The coordinator's fourth direction has been the provision of technical assistance in the establishment of new child care centers. In the fall of 1988, new child care centers will open in the new ARCO Arena, in a downtown housing project for the elderly (with the outdoor play area on the second floor roof), and in a specially designed building in a low-income neighborhood. A downtown child care center for sick children will open soon.

Possible future activities include enactment of an ordinance requiring developers to provide child care or pay a fee in lieu of child care and establishment of a Child Care Revolving Fund to receive and distribute public and private money for the expansion of child care facilities and programs.

Part of the impetus in Sacramento for moving this agenda is the support of Mayor Rudin who says, "For Sacramento to be an attractive city in the future, we must plan to include children and working families."

Juvenile Welfare Board
Pinellas County, Florida

Use of dedicated tax levy to enhance planning and increase services.

Contact:
James E. Mills, ACSW, Executive Director
Juvenile Welfare Board of Pinellas County
4140 49th Street North
St. Petersburg, FL 33709
(813) 521-1853

Pinellas County's Juvenile Welfare Board was established in 1945 as a separate, independent special district of local government with the authority to levy its own taxes. The taxes raised support a community wide needs assessment and programs to meet the needs identified.

In 1944, Juvenile Court Judge Lincoln Bogue's anger mounted each time he was confronted by his only option for housing abandoned, neglected and abused six- and seven-year-old children—the county jail. Even though other citizens shared his outrage, the County Commission refused to provide meaningful assistance. Their frustration led to a legislative solution—the proposed creation of a tax-supported, autonomous board to safeguard the rights, and serve the needs, of children. It was passed by the Flordia Legislature in 1945, subject to approval by local referendum. Eighty percent of the Pinellas voters approved the Juvenile Welfare Board Act in 1946. The Board was formed with an authorization to levy a tax of up to fifty cents per $1,000 of non-exempt Pinellas County property. It has operated continuously since that date.

The Juvenile Welfare Board's activities are directed by an eight-member board. The Juvenile Court Judge, the County Superintendent of Schools, and the Vice-Chairman of the County Commission serve as ex officio members. Five additional members are appointed for four-year terms by the Governor. The Board establishes policy, adopts the annual budget, votes the tax levy, provides oversight and employs the Executive Director. As a public entity, it must meet basic statutory requirements for fiscal accountability by public bodies, notice of public meetings, setting of tax rates and freedom of information. With few additional exceptions, it is free to organize itself and operate in the fashion it determines most expeditious. It has a high degree of autonomy and, in many ways, functions on a day-to-day basis more like a non-profit corporation or foundation than a traditional governmental agency.

The scope of responsibility of the Juvenile Welfare Board is very broad. While it is authorized to provide or fund a wide variety of services, it is mandated to provide none. Its only significant statutory limitation is a prohibition against funding any program or activity that is operated by the School Board — a clear reflection of the historic intent to maintain the maximum degree of autonomy from existing bodies and to protect the funding source from manipulation by other taxing bodies. The Board has, by policy, chosen not to fund income maintenance, emergency relief, recreational or health services programs, although the latter two may be funded when they are components of a broader, targeted social service program.

The Juvenile Welfare Board provides no direct services. It contracts with public and voluntary agencies for service delivery and has an extensive grant review and grant management program. All contracts have measurable goals and objectives and are monitored regularly for compliance. All projects are also required to include at least one outcome objective and a measure of client satisfaction. Program funding is classified into seven areas: child development, dependency, developmental disabilities, juvenile justice, mental health, substance abuse, and support services (such as information and referral). Allocations are made to address a prioritized array of problems identified as part of a cooperative, community wide needs assessment. Historically, there has been a commitment to funding prevention programs, with 21.26 percent classified as primary prevention, 35.5 percent as secondary prevention, 24.06 percent as tertiary prevention, and 19.18 percent as rehabilitation.

The budget for fiscal year 1987-88 is almost $14.8 million, based on a tax rate of almost forty-four cents (.4348) per thousand dollars of assessed valuation. (Some income is derived from interest, unspent funds from prior years, intergovernmental transfers, etc.) Approximately $12.7 million will be used for children's program services; approximately $1.5 million will be spent on administration (including community planning and staff training); and nearly $570,000 will go for other non-operating expenditures (e.g. capital outlays, mandated reserve funds, and prorated share of property assessment and tax collection costs).

The children's program services funds helped to pay for sixty-seven programs operated by thirty-seven different agencies that helped more than 150,000 children and parents in more than 22,000 families. Although one Florida official describes the Juvenile Welfare Board programs as "the icing on the cake, the things they don't have," the funding decisions are made through a community planning and prioritizing process that aims to fill in service gaps. The special taxing authority works in concert with the bodies responsible for mandated services. It allows more complementary things to happen. The availability of Juvenile Welfare Board funds has permitted an increase in the number of child care licensing workers in Pinellas County, for instance, beyond what state funds alone can provide in other counties. Establishing more school-age child care has been another effort. A third effort supports a city-run St. Petersburg program to work with truant children and their families. A fourth effort, the provision of family day care to children of homeless shelter residents, makes it possible for the parents to seek jobs and/or begin training.

Other programs focus on preventing children from getting into trouble in the first place, a media campaign to help prevent teen pregnancies, marriage and family counseling, runaway and emergency shelters, drug abuse counseling, mental health care and therapy for disabled children. An innovative program in the planning is Pinellas Village. It will be a community aimed at breaking the cycle of public dependency for motivated single parents by offering multiple services, such as housing, child care, and comprehensive family services. A similar program in Denver has reduced the percentage of familes receiving AFDC from 65 percent at the beginning of the clients' participation to 6 percent two years after leaving the community.

In addition to the grant management and general administrative functions, the Juvenile Welfare Board can provide other services, such as community planning, community problem solving, and service coordination. The seven Youth Services Advisory Committees, which include both service providers and community citizens, achieve significant service coordination and community involvement. The committees are organized around abuse, neglect and dependency; day care and early childhood; economic services; juvenile justice; legislation; mental health and substance abuse; and child health. Other activities include developing public policy positions, advocacy, new program development, ongoing needs assessment, technical assistance, training, and maintenance of a library and audio-visual center specializing in materials related to family and children's services and policies.

Advantages of the special taxing district include:

- establishment of a priority for children's services such that organizational and institutional energy goes into the management of resources, not the competitive scramble to get them;

- predictability of revenue permitting long-range planning;

- establishment of locally-based priorities; and

- combination of planning and coordinating responsibilities with funding such that there is the potential for development of a systematic approach to the design and delivery of services to children.

On the other hand, issues concerning the appropriateness of special taxing districts for human services, or any particular target group, include:

- funds from both the public and voluntary sectors that would ordinarily have gone to children's services will be diverted or replaced (While this has been the conventional wisdom for many years, a recent survey of resource allocations in comparable communities in Florida offers no supporting empirical evidence.);

- human services in a special taxing district may not get their share of general revenues when needs outstrip resources;

- taxing authority should never be lodged with a non-elected board which is not accountable to voters; and

- special taxing districts represent designated funding for narrowly defined purposes which prohibit testing the use of these public funds against the full range of public needs.

While arguments regarding the disadvantages of the special taxing district are not to be dismissed lightly, the advantages of a special taxing district for human services far outweigh the disadvantages. According to the Executive Director of the Pinellas County Juvenile Welfare Board, James Mills, "A wisely conceived, well-organized and managed special taxing district can provide a reliable source for meeting locally determined human service needs. Such an entity has the capability of empowering the local community to design and operate its own system of services...such new initiatives must be forthcoming no matter how unpopular they may initially be or how difficult their implementation might eventually prove."

Strategic Planning and Program Coordination

In 1986, the Florida Legislature passed a bill enabling other counties to establish Juvenile Welfare Boards. Later that same year, the voters of Palm Beach County passed a referendum to replicate the Juvenile Welfare Board model. Other counties are also studying this possibility.

The *St.Petersburg Times* notes that "the Juvenile Welfare Board has enjoyed unusual success in its mission...to provide alternatives to jail for children who go astray, to demonstrate to unhappy youngsters that someone cares and someone is willing to provide the security that may not be available at home, and to try to keep families together."

The experience of Pinellas County and the resulting passage of permissive legislation for such programs elsewhere in Florida demonstrate that the idea of dedicated taxation at the local level for children and youth programs is an example that may well be worth exploring in other locations.

James Mills' paper for a 1985 symposium of the National Association of Social Workers provided the framework for this profile.

References

Center for the Study of Social Policy. 1987. *The Annie E. Casey Foundation's New Futures Initiative: Strategic Planning Guide*. Washington, D.C.

Committee for Economic Development. 1987. *Children in Need: Investment Strategies for the Educationally Disadvantaged*. New York and Washington, D.C.

High/Scope Educational Research Foundation. "Good Preschools for Poor Children are Cost-Effective." Fact Sheet. Undated. Ypsilanti (MI):High/Scope Press.

Lansburgh, T.W. "Prevention: Not Closing the Barn Door After the Horse Has Run Away," *Monthly Memo*, Maryland Office for Children and Youth, V. 3, No. 3, August 1986.

Smith, T.W. 1987. "Public Attitudes Towards Cities and Urban Problems," Washington, D.C.: National League of Cities.

Chapter III

Child Care
by Marjorie K. Smith

By 1995, two-thirds of all children younger than age six and three quarters of school-age children are projected to have working mothers. Childrearing, in practice, has become a collaborative endeavor.
Deborah Phillips , Quality in Child Care, *1987*

The collaboration to which Phillips alludes is a necessity. Almost all of the mothers of these children are working, or will be working, to support their families. Whether the mother is the only wage earner in the family or shares that responsibility with a spouse, the children of these working families need care. As Phillips and Carollee Howes put it, "the question of whether or not children should be in child care has become obsolete."

Background

High-quality child care is a service of benefit to children, by providing care for them in their parents' absence and by encouraging each child's social, emotional, physical and intellectual growth; to parents, by making it possible for them to seek education or training, or to work; and to communities, by making it possible for parents to be productive members of their communities and by preparing children to become contributing members of society.

The *availability* of affordable high-quality child care is essential to all families. The degree to which *affordable* child care is available determines whether poor and moderate income families can achieve and maintain self-sufficiency. The degree to which affordable *high-quality* child care is available determines whether the children of these families will be able to begin school with the basic skills necessary to achieve success in school and society.

The Committee for Economic Development, a 45-year-old public policy research group whose 225 trustees are mostly top corporate executives, has urgently called for public attention to these needs. In its September 1987 report, *Children in Need: Investment Strategies for the Educationally Disadvantaged*, the Committee warns that the United States is creating "a permanent underclass of young people" who cannot hold jobs because they lack fundamental literacy skills and work habits. The report concludes that the most promising approach to solving the problem is "early and sustained intervention in the lives of disadvantaged children, both in school and out." Among the major recommendations is a call for high-quality child care arrangements for the children of poor working parents that stress social development and school readiness. Another recommendation calls for high-quality preschool programs for all disadvantaged three- and four-year-olds. These findings are supported by research that shows that early childhood intervention programs can have significant long-term effects, including decreased dropout rates and welfare dependency and increased school success.

Child care costs are high. For a parent with one child, working full time, using only one child care arrangement, the median weekly expenditure in 1984-85 was $42.70 (more than $2,000 per year) according to the U.S. Bureau of the Census. Costs vary by geographic region and by the quality of care. High-quality care (care similar to that delivered by the highly acclaimed Perry Preschool Program) costs nearly $4,000 per year. The American Federation of State, County, and Municipal Employees (AFSCME) reports that 40 percent of parents surveyed cannot afford their current child care arrangement or cannot afford the arrangement they would prefer.

The largest form of direct federal support for child care is the Social Services Block Grant. The Block Grant replaced the Social Services Program in 1982 and can be used for various child welfare and family support services. States choose which of the several eligible programs receive funds. Nationally, about 18 percent of the funds go to child care, but percentages vary greatly from state to state.

Federal funding for the Social Services Block Grant has failed to keep pace with inflation since 1981, and most states have not filled that growing gap. In fact, according to the Children's Defense Fund, twenty-nine states were spending less of their Block Grant funds for child care services in 1986 than in 1981, and overall state Block Grant expenditures for child care decreased approximately 12 percent over the same period. As a result, less than half the eligible families are served.

Not only do federal and state funds fall far short of meeting the need, but eligibility requirements are often in conflict with the program goals. For example, in some jurisdictions, publicly funded child care is available first for families in which the child or children are at risk of abuse. Insufficient public dollars may mean that families who need child care to obtain or maintain work or training are frozen out. Additional funding, or funding targeted to each of the groups, could alleviate the situation. In some localities, child care is available to families in which the potential wage earner is enrolled in a training or other educational program. However, if the child care subsidy ends when the training is completed, entry level workers are then faced with the burden of meeting child care costs on their own. Extended eligibility, on a sliding scale basis, could assist such families in maintaining consistent child care and in beginning to meet the financial responsibility of it. *Family Circle Magazine* in 1979 and a Lou Harris poll in 1987 indicate that the American public strongly supports the government subsidy that such a sliding scale would require.

Issues and Analysis

In addition to the predominant themes of affordability, quality and availability, it is important to note several specific issues in order to most appropriately develop and implement child care services.

First, child care does not mean solely center-based care for three- to-five-year-olds. **A variety of sponsoring organizations, facilities, and populations served characterize today's child care picture.** Child care is needed for infants, toddlers, and school-age children, as well as for preschoolers. The special care needs of very young children (feeding, diapering, health) and the logistical difficulties concerning school-age children (transportation, after-school activities) have contributed to a greater shortage of care for these populations than for preschoolers.

In addition, child care can take place in a variety of settings: a church or synagogue, a public or private school, a family day care home, the child's own home, a relative's home, or a specially designed building. These variants are not new, but it is now recognized that parental choice of location and age of entry for their children is vital and that positive results for children, their parents and their communities can be derived from any of them.

Second, the **lack of adequate salaries** for those caring for children constitutes a threat to the stability and quality of child care. The National Association for the Education of Young Children (NAEYC) reports that "child care staff earn less than zookeepers, parking lot attendants, leaf rakers, and amusement park attendants" and that "most child care staff earn a yearly income below the poverty level for a family of four." Study after study shows the value of retaining well-trained staff; yet child care salaries are so low that they discourage well-qualified workers from entering the field and actually encourage rapid turnover. Charlotte Zinsser's study of New York child care salaries points out the resulting dilemma:

> The Catch-22 is that we must either lower our standards in terms of the employees we hire or raise salaries to attract and retain staff. Lowering standards directly affects the quality of child care and puts children at risk. Raising salaries raises tuition beyond what parents can afford to pay without subsidization.

Employer involvement is a third issue. In the 1970s, employer involvement in child care meant a center at the work site for the children of employees, if it meant anything at all. Today, employers are involved in many other ways – lending technical assistance to child care programs in their communities, providing child care vouchers that employees can use in the child care programs of their choice, contributing to selected programs, purchasing reserved spaces for children of employees in area programs, providing resource and referral to employees so that child care may be obtained more easily, and offering employee benefits (such as flex-time and parental leave policies) that enable working parents to provide more of their own child care. "Although employer-assisted child care is rapidly increasing," reports NAEYC, "only an estimated 3,000 of the 6 million employers in this country provide such support to families." However, these creative efforts do signal the fact that the government is not the only major player, besides the family itself, in the child care delivery system. More employers will heed the encouragement from William J. Popejoy, Chairman and Chief Executive Officer of American Savings and Loan Association. "Good child care is good business. It improves employee loyalty, morale, productivity, and recruiting."

A fourth issue is **whether all the needs of the family are being addressed**. Some cities and states are shaping new programs to meet specific needs, such as preschool programs for four-year-olds or child care for children of teenage parents. To the extent that a preschool program takes up only part of a day, it may not meet the needs of parents who work a full day. To the extent that a program is custodial with primary attention to safety, sleep, and meals, it may not meet the child's need for attention to intellectual and social skills. And to the extent that a program is limited to the children of those who work, it may not reach all the poor children for whom early childhood opportunities have been proven to have the greatest promise in terms of payoffs later in life. Sharon Lynn Kagan, Yale University faculty member currently on leave to direct New York City's Project Giant Step, describes the best solution. "The distinction between child care as custodial and schools as educational is all but eliminated in descriptions of ideal programs. Scholars, practitioners, and policy makers all acknowledge that care and education go hand in hand in [high-] quality programs."

Various school districts and public and private agencies have shown themselves able to address these varying needs. It is possible for any agency to do it if sufficient commitment is given to the comprehensive needs of families: child care, wage earning, schooling, etc.

The fifth issue concerns the **appropriateness of the curriculum or programming**. Research concerning the Perry Preschool Program suggests that child-initiated learning is the key to having an effective, high-quality program. This means that teachers should take their direction from the children, rather than providing direction to them. The appropriate teacher role — to extend learning through appropriate questions and by providing appropriate books, toys, and equipment — is important, and it goes well beyond the passive or custodial role of a baby sitter. However, the child can and should lead the learning process. The teacher's role is to make sure that the environment is conducive to learning and that both physical and emotional resources are available.

The sixth issue is **the degree of regulation**. The federal government has moved away from its regulations. Therefore, it is up to the local or state government to focus both on minimal standards below which program operation is not permitted and on substantive standards that promote high-quality, effective programs. Some cities, like Denver, are rewriting child care regulations. Other cities, like Madison and Seattle, expect more from those programs that receive city funds and have established regulatory and/or monitoring requirements beyond those expected of state-licensed programs. In Dallas a different approach is being used. There, child care programs are eligible to receive incentives if they volunteer to participate in the accreditation program of the NAEYC. This highly regarded program, developed outside of government, is attracting many providers across the country that wish to meet standards of high quality. These city-based examples point out that regulations are necessary and they further point out the need and desire of city officials to have regulations that go beyond bare necessities.

Profiles

Many cities recognize the enormity of the problems faced by their residents who require access to affordable, high-quality child care in order to be productive members of society. These cities are taking steps to develop solutions to these problems. An increasing number of cities are adjusting the face of institutionalized city government by forming Offices for Children or hiring child care coordinators whose jobs are to assess the child care problems of city residents and to develop and implement program ideas and funding sources to help meet these needs. As a model for private sector employers, some cities are focusing on the child care needs of their own employees by offering flexible benefits or providing resource and referral services. Other cities are developing direct services for specific groups (e.g. infants, school children or sick children) or indirect services such as training for child care providers and underwriting of insurance costs. They may provide space for centers, require other property owners to provide space, or adapt zoning ordinances to encourage the development of child care programs. They may encourage programs which nurture parenting skills or provide for parental leave. Some of these city actions require no additional funds while some require new city expenditures or development of new and/or nontraditional funding sources.

This chapter presents several examples of innovative and successful activities and actions designed to meet the child care needs of city residents. The common thread in each of these profiles is that the community was able to identify specific needs and tailor solutions to the specific resources available to that community. In some of these, the private sector has identified problems, initiated programs to address the problems, operated the programs and funded them. In others, the city government is taking direct action. What all of the programs share is a commitment to meeting child care needs and the use of public, private, and/or family resources to meet those needs.

There are many cities, neighborhoods within cities, and counties surrounding cities that are addressing the child care needs of their residents. The few included in this chapter do not constitute, and are not meant to constitute, an exhaustive look at city government involvement in child care. Each profile was included because it represents an approach that can be adapted and applied to meet the needs of residents in other cities. These efforts were and are successful, not because of unique capabilities or circumstances, but because of commitment to meet the child care needs of the children and families. The profiles come from cities that represent a geographic and population mix to underscore the universality of the problem and of the solutions.

Seattle, Washington shows an example of a comprehensive approach to securing available, affordable and high-quality child care for its residents. Availability is addressed through incentives for development in the zoning ordinance and through space made possible by a school bond initiative. City-provided subsidies address affordability and quality through subsidy-related training and technical assistance services. Other programs such as parental leave and child care for sick children add to the breadth of Seattle's approach.

In Dallas, Texas, the mayor sparked the creation of a private, not-for-profit agency that has focused its energy on improving the quality of child care in Dallas through training and credentialing. This agency has expanded its efforts to include issues of availability with its involvement in an enhanced resource and referral system.

The city government is Denver, Colorado's largest employer and, as such, has attacked the problems of affordability and availability by offering a range of services to its own employees as a model for other employers in the city. The services include a child care resource and referral program, a vendor program, and salary redirection.

Madison, Wisconsin has had an extensive municipally funded child care program for many years and uses tuition subsidies to address not only affordability, but also quality.

Since 1975, Minneapolis, Minnesota has used Community Development Block Grant funds to subsidize home- and center-based child care. Although the funds are public and go through the Mayor's budget, the program is administered by a private, not-for-profit agency.

Amherst, Massachusetts is a small city that set out to address residents' concerns about child care and ended up with the creation of a Children's Services Department headed by a child care coordinator. Believing that the best way to address availability was through a resource and referral service, the city has embarked

Program Location	Population, Geography	Year Initiated	Budget	Municipal Involvement	Client Population	Services Provided
Comprehensive Child Care Program Seattle WA	493,846 northwest	1972	$1,700,000	part of city government; city funds	1,500 children subsidized 2,250 providers trained 2,610 hours of consultation	needs assessment; subsidies; zoning ordinances school-age child care facilities
Child Care Partnership Dallas, TX	904,599 south	1985	$350,000	mayoral task force; CDBG funds	incentives to 150 centers and 60 family day care homes; resource and referral to 2,600 families	promotion of high quality through funding and programmatic incentives
Office of Child Care Denver, CO	492,686 west urban	1986		city funding; mayoral task force	800 city employees	resource and referral; salary redirection; vendor program
City Day Care Program Madison, WI	170,616 upper midwest		$10,000 loan fund; $25,000 grants; $300,000 tuition	city funds; school board collaboration	centers	child care tuition; school-age child care development
Greater Minneapolis Day Care Association Minneapolis, MN	370,951 upper midwest	1975	$700,000	CDBG funds	40-45 centers	subsidy program
Children's Services Department Amherst, MA	33,229 east	1986	$31,000	part of town government		resource and referral planning

Programs Dealing with Child Care

upon an ambitious effort to survey child care needs of those who live and/or work in Amherst.

Concluding Remarks

The ways in which cities can be involved in child care are limited only by imagination and fiscal resources. Kahn and Kamerman, in *Child Care: Facing the Hard Choices*, point out that local initiatives are inventive in the wake of "federal privatization, decentralization, and deregulation." Cities can arrange for — or encourage the provision of — training for providers of child care. Cities can provide or stimulate subsidies to help parents meet the costs of child care. They can offer to their own employees — and encourage private employers to offer to theirs — on-site child care, vouchers to help parents meet the costs of child care, flexible benefit programs in which some child care costs are met, and parental leave and/or part-time employment policies to make it easier for parents to care for their children.

During the past decade, two significant changes have affected child care. There has been a dramatic increase in the need for child care — from infants to school-age children — because of the marked increase in the number of mothers in the work force. At the same time, the federal government, which had previously established minimum quality standards and provided funding for child care, began to withdraw its support. Some states have moved to fill the resulting vacuum. A few states, such as California and Massachusetts, have developed state-wide resource and referral services. Other states have provided funding for subsidies.

The basic unit for the delivery of child care is the family. When the social, educational, or economic climate makes it impossible for the family to provide continuous child care, the parents reach out to the immediate community for help. The community, by experiencing them first hand, can best identify the needs and assist in developing a wide range of alternatives to help families meet child care needs.

Some of the profiles in this chapter involve creating a climate in which the private sector can deliver child care services; zoning and regulations are two examples of this level of involvement. Here also it is important to mention resource and referral systems, which are most effective on a neighborhood or local level and which make it possible for the community to provide a direct service to the parents by helping them to identify what their child care options are and where those options can be found.

Cities can alter traditional administrative divisions of city government so that policies encouraging the development of child care programs can be carried out uniformly across department lines. Cities can encourage schools, recreation programs and other agencies to develop programs and policies supportive of child care. Cities can encourage the private sector to address local child care needs.

In addition, these profiles demonstrate that cities can learn innovative management of the state and federal funds that flow to the city. The funding streams ebb and flow; the cities must therefore be flexible and creative in the way they use the available resources to meet their child care needs.

The availability and affordability of high-quality child care programs at the local level are essential if our society is to meet the immediate and long-term needs of children, their families, and the communities in which they live. In the examples presented here, localities have identified specific community needs and set out to meet them.

References and resources are listed following the profiles on page 66.

This Seal of Quality is awarded by Child Care Partnership of Dallas to child care programs that meet the accreditation standards of the National Association for the Education of Young Children. Used with permission.

Comprehensive Child Care Program
Seattle, Washington

Multiple solutions to multiple needs.

Contact:
Billie Young, Child Care Coordinator
Division of Family and Youth Services
105 Union Street
Suite 160
Seattle, WA 98101
206/386-1143

Seattle is an example of a comprehensive approach to child care related issues. Through the commitment of the mayor, city council, and city department heads, assisted by a child care coordinator, Seattle has mounted a multi-faceted effort to meet the child care needs of city residents. Together, they have secured city funding and subsidies, used zoning ordinances and bond issues, developed innovative programs that have later been spun off to other agencies, and obtained cooperation from city departments that wouldn't ordinarily see child care as a priority (such as the Department of Construction and Land Use).

At the same time the state increased its efforts to support child care services, Seattle became aware of a gap between the supply of and the need for affordable child care within the city through a *Child Care Needs Assessment* conducted by the Seattle Department of Human Resources in August 1986. The city's interest in planning, supporting, and advocating a comprehensive child care system required answers to certain questions:

- How many children in Seattle need child care?

- Where do they live?

- What are their ages?

- What licensed care is available?

- How many children are in unlicensed settings?

- How affordable is child care in Seattle?

The answers, while specific to Seattle, are not unlike answers to similar questions in many other cities. After a long period of declining birth rates, birth rates in Seattle have risen about 20 percent since 1980. As a result, the preschool population has increased considerably. At the same time, there has been a major increase in the number of working women; an estimated 55.1 percent of all mothers of young children, and 71.9 percent of all mothers of school-age children, work.

In the state of Washington, there are three kinds of child care facilities:

- family day care homes, serving a maximum of six full-time and four part-time children (273 are licensed in Seattle);
- mini-centers, which may serve up to twelve children with two caretakers present (61 licensed in Seattle); and
- child care centers that serve more than twelve children and have a licensed capacity based on facility size and staffing (129 in Seattle).

Seattle's 463 facilities provide a combined total of 8,854 child care places, as compared with an estimated need of 22,929. Thirty-nine percent of the children who need care are receiving that care in licensed facilities.

The city has launched several programs that use city authority and resources, in combination with state and private resources, to better meet the need for more affordable, high-quality child care. The city has had a child care coordinator for fifteen years and has shown its commitment to comprehensive child care. But as the need for child care increased dramatically, the mayor formed an internal Day Care Task Force, composed of representatives from various city departments, to coordinate and track the various child care initiatives taking place under city auspices: the Department of Construction and Land Use's involvement in building permits and occupancy; the zoning staff's control of siting of new programs; and the Parks Department attention to the needs of latchkey children with after-school recreation programs, increased hours of operation and re-opening of playgrounds.

Of the many programs that show the creative way in which Seattle has attempted to meet child care needs, one of the most imaginative has to do with the construction of in-school child care space. In Seattle, the public school budget is separate from the mayor's budget. The schools, working to meet traditional school goals, had not focused on the child care needs of their constituency. The city, in an unusual move, spent $240,000 to provide two mobile units to be placed at two schools and to be used only for child care. Although the sites for these units were public schools, the child care was available all day, year round. This effort was so well received that when the school system proposed a $12 million school levy for repair and work on school buildings, $5 million was added for in-school child care space in fourteen elementary schools. Voters passed the bond levy overwhelmingly.

School children are bused in Seattle and do not necessarily attend their neighborhood schools. The school-age child care, however, is to be offered at the neighborhood school. At the end of the school day, school-age children will return to their neighborhoods, and those that participate in child care will do so at their neighborhood schools. The school experience reinforces integration efforts, while the child care program will help to reinforce a sense of community. In the fourteen projects made possible by the school levy, neighborhood needs assessments are being conducted so that the specific child care offered at each location best meets the needs of the surrounding community.

The city provides the staff for these projects, the school district provides the space, and the community will deliver the services either through not-for-profit or for-profit providers who can best meet the needs of the community. It is important to note that although the space is in school buildings, the need is in the neighborhood, and therefore, the care that will be delivered might be care for infants, toddlers, or preschoolers, alone or in combination, as well as for school-age children.

Zoning is another tool Seattle has used to increase the availability of space for child care. Incentives to builders for the provision of child care are typically in the form of building square footage bonuses. Generally, a developer is given the opportunity to include additional square footage, over that usually allowed within that particular zoning district. Two years ago, Seattle adopted a new downtown code providing strong incentives for developers to include free space for child care programs. Developers who incorporate child care space in new buildings get bonus square footage. Although bonuses are included for other public benefits, child care space has the highest bonus ratio of any public benefit feature. The developer is required to enter into a five-year lease with a child care provider before the certificate of occupancy is issued. The developer cannot charge rent but can assess a portion of the utility, insurance and maintenance costs. Twenty percent of those served by the provider must be from low-income families. Another code change now permits child care in the downtown area to be provided on floors above the ground level of a building.

Affordability and quality have been addressed through the Comprehensive Child Care Program. This program has two goals: to provide a subsidy so parents can work or participate in training and to inprove the quality of child care. The funding for the program comes from the Community Development Block Grant, the Private Industry Council (PIC)of the Job Training Partnership Act, United Way, the Washington State Department of Social and Health Services, and city general funds. Parents pay a fee of from 25 percent to 55 percent of the cost of care. The city offers support services, such as on-site training, technical assistance, and preventive health care. The city does the intake, but the child care is subcontracted to licensed providers, who are monitored by the city. The parents contact the providers themselves and may use either a list of contractors, or a voucher which permits the parent to purchase care at any licensed and insured program.

Seattle has also established many other policies and programs spanning the range of child care service. One of these is a parental leave policy that lets city employees use sick leave not only for their own illnesses, but also to care for a sick child; in addition, both maternity and paternity leaves are now allowed for new parents. The Child and Family Resource Center, established through city, foundation and corporation funds, provides training to child care providers, workshops for parents, and resource and referral information. The city also assists a pilot mini-center for homeless children from six shelters. The city, the school district, and the Chamber of Commerce helped establish a community consortium to focus on increasing before- and after-school child care options. Participants include employers, parents, school and government staff, parks and recreation experts and the business community.

Many of these projects reflect a strong commitment on the part of the city to use its resources to incubate programs, with the expectation that the city can spin them off as others express willingness to carry out the programs. The schools used a bond issue to pick up on the city's idea of enhancing school facilities for child care use. The Child and Family Resource Center will be spun off by 1988, and the before- and after-school consortium will become a non-profit corporation.

Another important lesson to be learned here is that just as problems are not necessarily city-wide, so, too, solutions may not be city-wide. It is more than possible that a neighborhood may get together – under the auspices of a community organization, a city councilman, a school, or an ad hoc group – to identify and set out to solve child care problems unique to that community. This approach is being implemented to make use of the in-school child care space created by the school levy.

With a comprehensive spread of policies and programs and a mix of federal, state, local and private funding, Seattle is demonstrating a strong commitment to improving the quality, availability and affordability of child care. Billie Young,

Child Care

Seattle's child care coordinator, points out that "the economic and quality issues which dominate the child care industry right now require formation of new partnerships and new solutions. The City of Seattle is, indeed, a new partner for child care, both in terms of funding and service development."

San Francisco offers another example of a city linking downtown office development to child care. Whereas Seattle's plan offers incentives, San Francisco's plan institutes requirements. In September of 1985, the Board of Supervisors adopted the Downtown Plan, which required that developers of all new office buildings or office renovations in excess of 50,000 square feet must either provide an on-site child care facility or make a contribution to a child care fund. Child care is actually addressed in three provisions:

- For the entire city, a requirement that developers of office projects over 50,000 square feet either set aside licensable space for a rent-free child care facility or contribute $1.00 per square foot to an Affordable Child Care Fund that will be used to expand the supply of child care for children from low- and moderate-income families.

- For the downtown business district only, a requirement that developers of office projects over 50,000 square feet provide information to the project's tenant work force on the availability of child care, parenting, and similar services designed to enable parents to select and use appropriate child care. Data about the child care needs of the people working in the building must also be collected by a project manager.

- For the entire city, a provision permitting exclusion of up to 6,000 square feet from the calculation of gross floor area if that space is devoted to on-site child care and if specific conditions assigned by the city are met.

Supervisor Nancy Walker sponsored the ordinance as part of the Downtown Plan, and it passed unanimously. Moira Shek So, Executive Director of the Mayor's Office of Community Development, which administers the legislation, reported that the provision has been extended to hotel development since November 1986. While most developers choose the fee option, several are working with community-based nonprofit corporations to develop child care facilities near their developments.

For more information, contact Moira Shek So, Executive Director, Mayor's Office of Community Development, City and County of San Francisco, 100 Larkin Street, San Francisco, CA 94102-4769; 415/558-2112.

Child Care Partnership of Dallas
Dallas, Texas

Public/private incentives to promote high-quality programs.

Contact:
Susan Taliaferro Lund, Executive Director,
Child Care Partnership of Dallas
1820 Regal Row
Suite #100
Dallas, TX 75235
214/638-5454

Public interest and governmental leadership can generate private efforts to resolve problems. In Dallas, through the work of the mayor, a private, not-for-profit agency was created that focused its efforts on improving the quality of child care. Starting with training and credentialing, this private agency has now joined forces with another to expand and enhance resource and referral.

State law requires public school pre-kindergarten programs in school districts having fifteen or more four-year-olds who are limited in their English proficiency, or who are from low-income families, as defined by the guidelines of the school lunch program. School districts with fewer than fifteen such students may provide pre-kindergarten programs if they choose to do so. Once all of the children in these two groups have been served, the district may include all other four-year-olds in the program. While the law creating the program requires a local match, it provides the maximum state support to those counties with the highest poverty rates. The program served 35,900 children in its first year, the 1985-86 school year. In addition, child care through the Social Services Block Grant served 14,943 children.

In the Dallas-Fort Worth area, 59.2 percent of all women were part of the work force in 1980. The median household income in 1980 was $18,853. Dallas has a city manager form of government with twenty-three departments.

In the fall of 1983, then mayor A. Starke Taylor made a bold statement in the course of naming a task force to recommend city policies for children. "Dallas shall be a model for the advocacy of excellence in the care of our children," Starke

50

said. "The mission...is to provide a plan...that creates an environment for children which assures their optimal growth and development and, in so doing, invests substantially in the future of Dallas."

In the spring of 1984, the task force, made up of eighty Dallas residents, including pediatricians, parents, attorneys, school board members, human service workers, and child care professionals, issued its recommendations. Heading the list was the creation of a non-profit agency to advocate high-quality child care. This recommendation led, in March 1985, to the start of the Child Care Partnership of Dallas, Inc. (CCPD). CCPD is an independent agency, with funds from the city, private foundations, local and national corporations and United Way. Of the $350,000 total budget, the city provides $40,000 through Community Development Block Grant funds. A recent city charter change will permit future consideration of the use of city funds.

The main program of CCPD is to encourage the voluntary participation of child care centers in meeting the standards of the highly-regarded accreditation program of the National Association for the Education of Young Children (NAEYC). These standards promote high-quality child care and go well beyond the minimum requirements of the Texas Department of Human Services for licensing centers and registering family day care homes. CCPD launched its Partnership Provider Program by offering incentives to child care providers who voluntarily go beyond the state's basic requirements and meet national standards for high quality. To those who participate in the self-study process (the first step in gaining NAEYC accreditation), CCPD offers discounts on accreditation fees, scholarships to teachers who are pursuing education, and on-site consultation to help them meet the requirements. When the self-study is complete, centers are eligible to apply for CCPD grants to acquire materials and equipment necessary for them to eliminate any deficiencies discovered in their programs. An additional incentive-based component of this project is the offering of workshops during the year at Dallas Community Colleges for teachers and directors. These workshops focus on specific criteria needed for accreditation. CCPD will launch a similarly structured accreditation program aimed at recognizing and improving quality among family day care providers in 1988. This program will be based on criteria developed by NAEYC through its Child Development Associate Certificate Program.

In addition to this focus on improving quality, a focus on availability has been strengthened. "In Dallas the percentage of women who are working is second only to that of Washington, D.C.," said Susan Lund, Executive Director of CCPD. "Among this female work force, 80 percent will have at least one child during their working career. The need for child care is escalating, and finding suitable child care can be a big problem for parents." In June 1987, CCPD joined forces with Child Care Dallas (CCD) to expand the hours and lower the cost to parents of CCD's existing computerized resource and referral hot line, CHILD CARE ANSWERS.

CHILD CARE ANSWERS is free to parents the first time they call. "Sometimes the first search does not fulfill the parents' requirements because they are unable to find openings in the child care programs, or they want to specify different criteria," said Roberta Bergman, Executive for Resource Development for Child Care Dallas. "Therefore, a second search may be required." The second search costs $10.00 for a family with an income greater than $15,000; it is free for families with incomes less than $15,000. Child Care Dallas has been serving child care needs of the Dallas area for eighty-six years and operates seven child care centers and more than sixty family day care homes. Manned by telephone counselors who find out what parents want concerning child care cost, location, and hours, the parents are then sent fact sheets on the centers and homes which match those requirements. The parents are urged to visit the programs themselves to underscore the program's philosophy of parental responsibiity for selecting child care services. The computer information is provided without recommendation or endorsement. Additional services, such as checking for vacancies in particular programs, cost an additional fee, adjusted according to family income.

Child care affordability is addressed by CCPD when it acts as an advocacy organization at the state level with a coalition of more than 100 concerned groups and agencies convened by United Way of Texas. The efforts of this Child Care Working Group were successful during the past legislative session when the line was held on funding cuts for child care for low-income families.

In tying incentives to the innovative NAEYC accreditation process, Dallas has made a major step toward improving the quality of child care for its residents.

Office of Child Care Initiatives
Denver, Colorado

The city as model employer.

Contact:
Martha Daley, Director
Office of Child Care Initiatives
1625 Broadway
Suite 2535
Denver, CO 80202
303/892-0731

Denver shows how a city can offer a range of child care and family-oriented services to its own employees. A child care resource and referral system, a vendor program, and voluntary salary redirection offer examples of ways in which city governments can meet the child care needs of their own employees and serve as role models for other employers in their areas.

The city's efforts came in the wake of the state reductions in child care assistance as the result of Gramm-Rudman cuts in the Social Services Block Grant. Colorado eliminated child care assistance for low-income families enrolled in two-year education programs (allowing no more than twelve months of child care support) and reduced child care expenditures for children in protective services and for those "at risk" of being placed in foster homes.

In August 1986, there were 871 centers (150 in Denver) with a licensed capacity of 47,878 and 5,529 family day care homes (680 in Denver) with a licensed capacity of 28,284.

Soon after being elected in 1984, Mayor Federico Peña convened a forum on women's issues, which listed child care as one of the top issues of Denver women. Later in 1984, a child care forum recommended child care for city employees. In May 1985, the mayor established a fifteen-member Child Care Advisory Committee, composed of child care providers and consumers, business people, and representatives of the PTA, schools, city council, mayor, and city employees. A needs assessment, conducted from May to December, showed that 84 percent of all employees favored "an effort on the part of the City and County of Denver to address child care issues." More men than women responded, and even those who did not have children recognized that child care affects work performance and productivity.

"Child care affects people who don't even have kids," said Martha Daley, Director of the Office of Child Care Initiatives. "It's a work productivity issue because supervisors and co-workers understand that they, too, are adversely affected when employees can't find quality, affordable child care."

In April 1986, the city government, Denver's largest employer, established its Office of Child Care Initiatives to deliver services to city employees. Since then, approximately 800 city employees have used services including a child care resource and referral system, a vendor program, a salary redirection plan, and parent education seminars.

The resource and referral system refers parents who call for help in finding child care arrangements to community resources and sends the parents information on such child-care-related topics as choosing child care and the importance of using licensed child care. Packets on summer camps and before- and after-school child care are part of this service. This resource and referral system for city employees has helped in developing a broader city-wide system.

The vendor program provides for a discount, usually 10 percent, on child care costs at approximately fifty Denver child care facilities with which the city has signed agreements. The services provided by these facilities (both for-profit and not-for-profit facilities) include center- and home-based child care, nanny services, and sick child care. The providers of the services get free marketing, and city employees get the 10 percent discount. Both sides reap real benefits from the city's small investment in drawing up and mailing a standard agreement.

Denver is also enrolling employees in a Salary Redirection Plan, a U.S. Internal Revenue Service regulated program that allows participating workers to redirect a portion of their salary (up to a maximum of $5,000 annually) to child care expenses. Since the earned salary has been redirected before the employee receives it, employees do not have to pay taxes on the part of their incomes that are redirected to child care. Therefore, child care purchased in this fashion is more affordable. The city also saves dollars through this plan because it does not pay social security or withholding taxes on the money which is redirected for such child care expenses.

In addition to these services provided for city employees, the Office of Child Care Initiatives has been involved in streamlining the child care licensing procedures.

Child Care

The Office has initiated communication among city agencies that license child care facilities, encouraged the zoning agency to request a code change to allow conformity across city districts relative to outdoor requirements for child care facilities, and collaborated with the health agency in writing an ordinance with clear and consistent child care licensing requirements. The Office has been increasing public awareness of child care issues and has been encouraging high-quality child care through its participation in community organizations that promote employer-related child care.

The programs for city employees are still so new that it is impossible to know the extent to which the city's example will be followed by other employers. However, two Denver employers — RTD Transportation and Coors Brewing — have already contracted for their own resource and referral services for their employees.

The City of San Diego provides another example of how the city as an employer can be a model for other employers. The city offers two forms of child care assistance for city employees: reimbursement of actual expenditures based on certain parameters and discounted rates at a city-sponsored facility. Special leave and part-time work opportunities are also available. For further information, contact Ross McCollum, Community Program Administrator, City of San Diego, 1200 Third Avenue, Suite 924, San Diego, CA 92101; 619/236-5644.

City Day Care Program
Madison, Wisconsin

City provision of child care tuition and impact on child care quality .

Contact:
Dorothy Conniff
Office of Community Services
Room 513
210 Martin Luther King, Jr. Boulevard
Madison, WI 53710
608/266-6520

Tuition subsidies can affect not only the affordability of child care, but its quality as well. Madison has had an extensive municipally funded program for many years, and its City Day Care Program offers an example of the use of public funds to improve and maintain the quality of child care programs.

Between 1981 and 1986, the number of children receiving child care through Social Services Block Grant funds rose from 7,774 to 13,000. That increase, however, was not enough to permit all who need publicly subsidized child care to receive it. In August 1986, Wisconsin reported 1,227 child care centers with a licensed capacity of 43,500 and 2,986 family day care homes.

Counties in Wisconsin set the maximum reimbursement rates for preschool, infant/toddler and school-age care using guidelines established by the state.

Madison was one of the first cities to take the initiative to establish an extensive municipally funded (using local tax dollars) child care program, linking tuition subsidies and the quality of care. More than $300,000 of the city money goes for tuition subsidies for parents; certification, training and technical assistance for child care programs; and school-age child care.

If family income is too high to qualify for county assistance, the city government can provide financial assistance on a sliding scale to help eligible parents pay for child care. That assistance can be provided for infant, preschool or school-age care while a parent works, is looking for work, is attending training or school (up to two years above high school) or to meet a child's special needs.

Child Care

For a family of four with a monthly gross income up to $1,399, full tuition is available; partial assistance is available for those with higher incomes.

The primary goal of the City Day Care Program is to improve and support the quality of child care in the city. As part of that effort, city tuition aid can only be spent in city-certified programs. City certification is in addition to licensing by the State of Wisconsin. To support and improve the quality of child care programs, the city employs three child care specialists who offer training and technical assistance to help them meet the city's standards. If programs need assistance to meet the quality standards, they may use the city's small grants program, which provides about $22,000 each year.

In 1983, the Joint Alternative Child Care Committee was established to develop programs to address the availability of school-age child care. By the end of 1985, the number of children enrolled in before-school, after-school and vacation programs more than doubled, according to the Office of Community Services. Child care designed specifically for school-age children is available in child care centers, schools, and other facilities. Some family day care homes and child care centers without special school day programs also absorb school-age children — often kindergarten and first grade children who have young siblings in the program already.

The marked increase in services would not have been possible without two steps taken by the Board of Education. It adopted a statement of support for school-age programs in school buildings, and it demonstrated its commitment by reducing the rental fee for space. Along with the support of the Board of Education, other factors responsible for the increase included the responsiveness of agencies providing school-age care to expand their services, the willingness of community agencies to develop innovative programs, the support of school principals in finding space for school-age programs within crowded buildings, and the availability of funds to help start innovative programs. The city has also established a $10,000 revolving loan fund.

About 800 children were being served in after-school child care programs by the end of 1985; about 500 were enrolled in vacation programs; and about 150 were in before-school child care programs. The need for before-school, vacation, and summer care for school-age children is far from being met, but the city is currently focusing its attention on these areas.

Three innovative school-age child care programs in Madison bear mentioning. One is FLIP, the Friendly Listener Intergenerational Program, developed by the Retired Senior Volunteer Program (RSVP). Senior volunteers provide a telephone reassurance for children who return to an empty home after school. Another is a drop-in program in which school-age children can be registered, run by United Neighborhood Centers. Another program, Kids' Day Out, provides a variety of activities for children on teachers' in-service training days.

Joint and separate endeavors by city government, the school system, and private agencies have made child care more affordable and more available in Madison, and improved its quality as well.

Greater Minneapolis Day Care Association
Minneapolis, Minnesota

Innovative management of CDBG funds for child care.

Contact:
Dale Anderson, Executive Director
Greater Minneapolis Day Care Association
1006 West Lake
Minneapolis, MN 55408
612/823-7243

Community Development Block Grant (CDBG) funds have been used by cities and states in a number of ways to meet child care needs. In Minneapolis, CDBG funds have been used since 1975 to subsidize child care centers and family day care homes. And although the funds are public funds, the Minneapolis program has been administered by a private, not-for-profit agency.

In 1980, there were 164,731 females over the age of fifteen living in Minneapolis, 58 percent of whom were in the work force. Of women with children under six years of age, 53 percent were in the work force.

In 1985, there were 665 licensed child care facilities in Minneapolis with a licensed capacity of 9,666. Among these facilities were 540 family day care homes, 73 full day child care centers, 39 half day child care centers, 2 Head Start programs and 11 public school latchkey sites. Three child care programs exist to care for ill children. There are approximately 30 child care programs not subject to licensing (such as those using a Montessori philosophy and some of those in public schools) and an unknown number of unlicensed family day care settings.

Since 1975, Minneapolis has used Community Development Block Grant funds to subsidize tuition at child care programs. The CDBG program permits any city to use up to 15 percent of its CDBG funds for human services. Minneapolis has consistently spent up to that allowable amount. The annual expenditure has been between $700,000 and $800,000. The process demonstrates a high degree of cooperation between the city and the private sector, with each depending upon the other for specific expertise and resources.

Children, Families & Cities

The Greater Minneapolis Day Care Association (GMDCA) works with the city to assess need, and the city balances the need for child care against other needs it must meet. Then, GMDCA uses its specific skills to evaluate proposals from child care providers to identify those that best meet the needs identified by the city and GMDCA.

In May of each year, GMDCA submits an umbrella proposal to the city, according to the association's executive director. About one month later, the association makes a presentation to a citizens review committee that also hears all other human service requests. This committee makes recommendations to the mayor and city council.

In August, the mayor submits his city budget to the city council which reviews it and votes on it in late November or early December. The mayor's recommendations always include an amount for child care and, generally, the final amount received is very close to what the mayor proposed. The association actively provides information to the mayor and the city council throughout the process.

In early winter, the association invites child care programs to submit requests. At the same time, the association forms a citywide, community-based committee that sets provider requirements and then reviews and makes recommendations on grants. For 1987-88, the requirements include: stability of the program; provision of services which are difficult to find in the community such as infant care and evening, night or weekend care; care for special needs children; effective use of CDBG funds to supplement, not replace, other fee subsidy programs; fair recruitment and selection of eligible families to benefit from the grant; and effectiveness of affirmative action in staffing decisions. The grant requests are generally submitted in mid-January. In March, after reviews and interviews, the committee submits its recommendations to the GMDCA board for final action.

The grant request must relate to providing financial assistance to low-income families. GMDCA monitors the spending of those funds to insure that the target population does receive the services. Some of the funds, however, are allocated to other agencies to provide supportive services such as training, technical assistance, and resource and referral. Use of funds for these purposes does not have to be specifically related to income. Support services that have been funded with CDBG money also include a toy lending library, family day care field trips, child care for sick children, an infant care incentive program (providing funds for equipment and facility changes to accommodate infants) and newsletters. A supplemental allocation of $50,000 in CDBG funds is being used by the association to recruit family day care providers to take care of children of teenage parents.

Child Care

GMDCA has been successful in negotiating with suburban municipalities within the county. There are now fourteen cities that allocate CDBG funds to be used by the association to provide child care subsidies to their residents.

Each year, forty to forty-five centers and family day care homes receive grants for subsidies. This effort is successful in using public resources and private expertise in making child care more affordable for city residents.

Children's Services Department
Amherst, Massachusetts

Resource and referral.

Contact:
Roy Rosenblatt, Director
Amherst Children's Services Department
Town Hall
4 Boltwood Avenue
Amherst, MA 01002-2351
413/253-5771

Amherst offers an example of the many implications of a resource and referral system. Out of the results of a community survey came not only a decision to implement a resource and referral system, but also the creation of a Children's Services Department to administer such a program and a commitment to determine where and what kinds of child care would be needed to meet the community's needs.

Massachusetts, a state with a strong economy, has made remarkable progress during the past several years. The Children's Defense Fund points out that Massachusetts not only provided child care to 30 percent more children in 1986 than in 1981, but also approved salary initiatives totaling more than $9 million for 1985 and 1986 to help struggling child care providers. The state has recognized the importance of child care in the design of its ET (Employment Training) Choices program, guaranteeing support for adequate child care to AFDC mothers while they are in training and as they move into the work force. The state has spent $18 million to provide vouchers for child care for more than 5,000 children whose parents are participating in this program. The projection for 1987 is $20 million to serve 6,000 children. Parents receive vouchers to be used in licensed child care facilities. Child care assistance is continued for one year after a parent secures gainful employment.

Massachusetts has allocated $1.2 million to fund ten non-profit agencies to provide, on a regional basis, resource and referral services, consumer education, compilation of data on supply and demand, resource development, technical assistance and child care training. This regional approach is based on the assumption that child care is a local service. These resource and referral agencies are mandated to become the hub of a support system that matches supply and demand and offers the supportive services without undermining provider autonomy or parental choice.

The Massachusetts Education Improvement Bill authorizes funds for a wide range of programs for young children. The legislation authorizes up to $20 million that will go to schools to expand or set up pre-kindergarten programs for three- and four-year-olds, to expand kindergarten programs, and to sponsor child care programs that meet the needs of the community. A school district applying for funds must establish a local advisory board composed of representatives from local community agencies concerned with the welfare of young children. Such representatives must include a member of the local resource and referral agency and others with expertise in the care and education of young children.

Between 1981 and 1986, total expenditures on child care using Social Services Block Grant funds went from $43 million to $68.5 million, an increase of 59.4 percent. (These figures do not include funds for the Massachusetts' Department of Public Welfare child care voucher project or for the Education Improvement initiatives described above.)

Massachusetts' Industrial Finance Agency, which issues the state's industrial revenue bonds, has set up a $750,000 pilot loan fund for starting up, renovating, and/or constructing child care facilities. The maximum loan size is $250,000. New England Telephone matched this amount, offering grants over the next three years to non-profit child care centers to help pay for capital improvements and equipment. To provide technical assistance to employers interested in addressing the child care needs of their employees, an Office of Child Day Care has been established within the Executive Office of Economic Affairs.

Amherst includes within its boundaries both the University of Massachusetts and Amherst College. Within the town, there are currently 142 family day care slots; center-based child care provides 262 full-day slots and 170 part-day slots. Four years ago, the Town of Amherst conducted a survey to determine how best to address citizen's concerns about child care. Although there was some support for using town funds for direct services, the town officials decided that resource and referral services would help to solve some of the existing problems with availability of child care and that a specialized department within the town government would be the best way to offer the services, rather than using one of the state-funded programs. The Amherst Children's Services Department was established with a child care coordinator to head it on a temporary basis. The position was made permanent at a town meeting in 1986.

The Children's Services Department, which has a current budget of $31,000, has been in existence for less than a year; it has had time only to start the process of developing a comprehensive service delivery plan that will guide its efforts to coordinate and expand high-quality programs for children and their families. In conjunction with the local Early Childhood Advisory Committee mandated under the state's new Education Improvement Bill, the Department first conducted a survey/needs assessment of families with children between two and six years of age; a subsequent survey is determining the needs of families with children under two years of age, including whether there is a shortage of care for infants and toddlers.

The cooperative nature of the survey process not only permits the school district to meet state requirements, but also provides the Children's Services Department with some of the basic documentation needed as it searches for both state and private funds to meet the child care needs of the community. One aspect of availability is that the true number of families looking for child care in Amherst is substantially greater than that indicated by the population figures because many families work in Amherst that do not live there.

Availability is a major problem in Amherst, but affordability is also an issue. The Children's Services Department has concluded that the shortage of programs for infants and toddlers is due in large part to the high costs of providing these services. For family day care, the average rate is $4,800 per year; center-based care for preschool children is approaching $5,200 per year. Statistics from the most recent survey indicate that more than 30 percent of Amherst's families earn $20,000 or less per year, confirming the department's opinion that many families may have difficulty in affording child care. Department activities to address affordability include subsidizing after-school child care slots (by providing approximately $10,000) and administering a small fund used to reserve slots for town employees. The Children's Services Department, in conjunction with the Amherst Planning Department, has applied to the State Executive Office of Community Development for partial funding to construct a community child care center. This facility, to be built on town land, would be a partnership between the state, the town and local employers interested in providing child care assistance to their employees.

Child Care

In a small city like Amherst, it has been possible for the town government to identify a community concern about the need for affordable child care and to take steps to focus attention on the issue by hiring one staff person who has been able to work to establish relationships with providers, parents and private agencies. He has also become involved in the developing network of child care coordinators in cities throughout the country. The resulting exchange of information permits Amherst to benefit from the experience of many cities in attempting to meet child care needs.

Further information about resource and referral agencies and services can be obtained from the National Association of Child Care Resource and Referral Agencies, 2116 Campus Drive, S.E., Rochester, MN 55904; 507/287-3020.

References

Ad Hoc Day Care Coalition. 1985. *The Crisis in Infant and Toddler Child Care*. Washington, D.C.

American Federation of State, County, and Municipal Employees. 1987. *America's Child Care Needs: The 1987 ASCFME National Secretary's Week Opinion Poll*. Washington, D.C.

Berrueta-Clement, J.R., Schweinhart, L.J., Barnett, W.S., Epstein, A.S., and Weikart, D.P. 1984. *Changed Lives: The Effects of the Perry Preschool Program on Youths Through Age 19*. Monographs of the High/Scope Educational Research Foundation, 8. Ypsilanti (MI): High/Scope Press.

Blank, H., and Wilkins, A. 1985. *Child Care: What Priority?* Washington, D.C.: Children's Defense Fund.

Committee for Economic Development. 1987. *Children in Need: Investment Strategies for the Educationally Disadvantaged*. New York and Washington, D.C.

Friedman, D.E. 1987. *Family-Supportive Policies: The Corporate Decision Making Process*. New York: The Conference Board.

Galinsky, E. 1986. *Investing in Quality Child Care: A Report for AT&T*. Short Hills (N.J.): AT&T.

Kagan, S.L., "Schooling for Four Year Olds Debate: Implications for Child Care," *Child Care Information Exchange*, September 1986, p. 19.

Kahn, A.J. and Kamerman, S.B. 1987. *Child Care: Facing the Hard Choices*. Dover (MA).: Audubon House.

Kamerman, S.B. and Kahn, A.J. 1987. *The Responsive Workplace, Employees and a Changing Labor Force*. Irvington (N.Y.): Columbia University Press.

Levine, J.A. 1978. *Day Care and the Public Schools: Profiles of Five Communities*. Newton (MA).: Education Development Center.

National Association for the Education of Young Children. 1986. "NAEYC Position Statement on Developmentally Appropriate Practices in Programs for Four and Five Year Olds." Washington, D.C.

National Association for the Education of Young Children. Undated. "Where Your Child Care Dollars Go." Washington, D.C.

National Black Child Development Institute. 1987. *Safeguards: Guidelines for Establishing Programs for Four-Year-Olds in the Public Schools*. Washington, D.C.

Phillips, D.A. (Ed.) 1987. *Quality in Child Care: What Does Research Tell Us?* Washington, D.C.: National Association for the Education of Young Children.

Zinsser, C. 1986. *Day Care's Unfair Burden: How Low Wages Subsidize a Public Service*. New York: The Center for Public Advocacy Research.

Resources

Child Care Action Campaign: The Child Care Action Campaign is a coalition of leaders from government and industry, national organizations, labor, the media, women's groups, and academia. The Child Care Action Campaign's long-range goal is to set in place a national system of high-quality affordable child care, using all existing resources, public and private. Contact: Barbara Reisman, Executive Director, 99 Hudson Street, Room 1233, New York, New York 10013; 212/334-9595.

School-Age Child Care Project: The School-Age Child Care Project promotes the availability of school-age child care across the country through a regular newsletter, books, and technical assistance. Contact: Michelle Seligson, Director, c/o Center for Research on Women, Wellesley College, Wellesley, MA 02161; 617/235-0320.

Children's Defense Fund: The Children's Defense Fund exists to provide a strong and effective voice for the children of America, who cannot vote, lobby, or speak for themselves. Concerning child care, CDF tracks federal and state expenditures, advocates policy, and currently devotes substantial attention to the federal Act for Better Child Care. Contact: Helen Blank, Director of Child Care and Family Support Services, 122 C Street NW, Washington, DC 20001; 202/628-8787.

National Association for the Education of Young Children: The National Association for the Education of Young Children is a nonprofit membership organization dedicated to improving the professional practice of early childhood education with more than 300 affiliate groups in communities across the country, public policy information on efforts at all levels of government, and the NAEYC Information Service (a computer-based centralized source of information sharing and collaboration). Contact: Marilyn Smith, Executive Director; 1834 Connecticut Avenue NW, Washington, DC 20009; 202/232-8777 or 800/424-2460.

The Child Care Employee Project (CCEP): CCEP advocates for improved wages, status, and working conditions for child care providers in the belief that such improvement will enhance quality by improving staff morale and performance and by reducing turnover. CCEP provides resources, training, consultation, and a newsletter. Contact: Marcie Whitebook, Executive Director, CCEP, P.O. Box 5603, Berkeley, CA 94705; 415/653-9889.

National Black Child Development Institute: The National Black Child Development Institute works to improve the quality of life for black children and youths. It focuses on issues of health, education, child welfare, and child care. A network of NBCDI affiliates in cities across the country serves as a catalyst for change at the local level. Contact: Evelyn K. Moore, Executive Director, 1463 Rhode Island Avenue NW, Washington, DC 20005; 202/387-1281.

Ad Hoc Association of City and County Child Care Coordinators: The Ad Hoc Association of City and County Child Care Coordinators informally shares information about local government involvement in child care activities and policies. Contact: Nancy Noble, Child Care Coordinator, City of Irvine, 2815 McGaw, P.O. Box 19575, Irvine, CA 92713; 714/660-3995.

The Child Care Law Center: The Child Care Law Center recently published *Planning for Child Care,* edited by Abby J. Cohen, which explores land use planning and development as they relate to child care. Contact: Child Care Law Center, 625 Market Street, Suite 915, San Francisco, CA 94105; 415/495-5498.

This poster from Massachusetts attracts both employers and high school seniors who want to participate in the effective school-to-work transition program of Jobs for Bay State Graduates. Used with permission.

Chapter IV

Youth Employment
by Marcia I. Cohen

> *"I didn't finish high school. I was a dropout. Before I went to the program I wasn't doing nothing, just hanging out with the fellows. No money in my pocket and nothing to do with my time. I got my GED at the program and they got me a job at the hotel. Now I'm attending Northeastern Illinois University, majoring in electronics. I want to be an electronics engineer technician. That's my field now."*
>
> *Frankie Sangster, Bellman, Ritz-Carlton Hotel*
> *and former client at Jobs for Youth (Chicago)*

Frankie Sangster and thousands of other teenagers have been reconnected to the worlds of work and school through a variety of youth employment, education, and training programs operating in cities throughout the country. Employment professionals who work with these youths have found that dropouts and youths at risk of dropping out can be turned around with support, attention, rigorous programs, and a lot of effort.

The employment picture for today's youth, however, is not all that bright. The population and economy are changing. There is a growing disparity between poor, minority youth, however, and the rest of the population. Dropout rates among inner city youths are skyrocketing while there is a shortage of alternative schools and local skills training programs to reach at-risk youths. The problem is getting so severe that the Committee for Economic Development recently said:

> "The United States is creating a permanent underclass of young people for whom poverty and despair are life's daily companions. These are youths who cannot hold jobs because they lack fundamental literacy skills and work habits....They cannot attain the living standard of most Americans because they are trapped in a web of dependency and failure."

Add to this the fact that manufacturing jobs, formerly a common entry to the workplace for unskilled youths, are rapidly disappearing from our inner cities while minority and immigrant populations there are rapidly increasing, and it is easy to see that cities are faced with a persistent teenage employment problem requiring a variety of solutions.

The challenge to bring these youths back into mainstream society is difficult, but many programs have turned young, unproductive lives into helpful, constructive ones at small cost, especially compared to the cost to society of doing nothing.

Background

The gap between the unemployment rates for youths and the rate for adults has widened over the past thirty years. From 1949 to 1980, the unemployment rate for white male teens remained about three times greater than that for adult males. The unemployment rate for 16 to 24 year olds rose from 8.2 percent in the years from 1947 to 1957 to 10.4 percent in the 1960s, 12.6 percent in the 1970s, and in August 1987 stood at 16 percent.

Despite the persistence of the overall teenage unemployment rate, the primary problem is the concentration of high youth unemployment among black and Hispanic youths and disadvantaged youths. The black youth unemployment rate has consistently been more than twice that for white youths, although it has been declining recently. The black youth unemployment rate stood at 40 percent in 1975, peaked at nearly 50 percent in 1982, and stands today at 29.2 percent, the lowest unemployment rate for black teens since October 1973. Despite this posi- tive downward trend, white teenagers are still twice as likely to be working as black teens. The most recent U.S. Bureau of Labor Statistics data show that 32.5

percent of black and 8.6 percent of Hispanic teenagers are employed, compared to 50.6 percent of white teens.

Research has found that prolonged periods of unemployment during youth increase the probability of long-term low earnings, low self image, and frequent unemployment as an adult. Statistics showing that joblessness among young black adults has increased bear this out. Between 1955 and 1982, joblessness among black men 25 to 34 years of age rose from 15 percent to 23 percent.

The prime reason for youth unemployment is school failure as exemplified by dropping out of high school. The unemployment rate for high school dropouts is two to three times greater than for high school graduates. Dropouts are more likely to be unemployed and more likely to get involved with crime or depend on welfare during their lifetimes:

- In 1985, 29.4 percent of the students entering high school did not graduate.

- In 1987, nearly one million youths will leave the nation's schools without graduating, and another 700,000 will be as deficient in skills and work habits as dropouts. Disadvantaged students are three times more likely to drop out of school as students who are more well off. The more poor children in a school, the higher the school's dropout rate: urban schools with less than 20 percent poor students had a 13 percent dropout rate; those with more than 50 percent poor students had dropout rates of 30 percent or more (Hahn and Danzberger, *Dropouts in America*, 1987).

- In inner cities, dropout rates for black students are as high as 45 percent; for Hispanics, from 50 percent to 80 percent.

- Poor, minority students accounted for 65 percent of unemployed youth but only 6.5 percent of the youth population in 1979.

National dropout rates differ significantly by race as well: 13 percent of white students dropped out in 1985 compared to between 12 and 24 percent of black students and 40 percent of Hispanic students. In some districts, up to 75 percent of Puerto Rican students drop out and 48 percent of Native Americans.

In 1985, according to the U.S. General Accounting Office (GAO), 4.3 million sixteen-to-twenty-four-year-olds (13 percent of that age group) dropped out of school. Dropout rates are greater for males than for females: 16 percent of the young men between eighteen and nineteen years of age were dropouts compared to 12 percent of similarly aged women. Dropout rates also differ by region of the country: southwestern states had the highest dropout rates, at 21 percent, compared to 18 percent in the northeast, 11 percent in the southeast, and 9 percent in the northwest. Rates in larger cities are twice those in smaller cities (25 percent compared to 13 percent).

For girls, pregnancy, in addition to poverty and race, is a major reason for dropping out of school. The high rate of unmarried motherhood among young black women contributes to their low employment levels. In 1979, 31 percent of black and 7 percent of white girls between 18 and 21 years of age were unmarried mothers. However, only 20 percent of the black unmarried mothers had jobs, compared to 50 percent of all other young black women.

Illiteracy and functional illiteracy also go hand-in-hand with the dropout problem. A national study by the Congressional Budget Office in 1982 estimated that 12 percent of all high school students cannot read. In the mid 1970s, however, a national test of seventeen-year-olds found that 42 percent of black and 9 percent of white youths were functionally illiterate.

Other reasons for dropping out of school include poor grades, dislike for school, alienation from peers, marriage, or going to work to support the family. Hahn and Danzberger characterize the typical dropout as an underachiever, from a household where there is little support for homework or academic achievement, and often with poor basic skills. They emphasize that with early intervention, most dropouts could have been helped.

Demographic changes taking place today will drastically affect the workforce. Over the next ten to fifteen years, the number of young people in the workforce will shrink by two-fifths. More than 75 percent of the workforce in the year 2000 is already at work today. It is estimated that the population of sixteen- to-twenty-four-year-olds will decline about 7 million during this decade from 38.4 million in 1980 to 31.5 million in 1990. However, there will be an increase in the number of disadvantaged youth, since youth populations are increasing among minorities. While only 7.5 percent of the white population is under eighteen years old, 38 percent of the black population, and 42 percent of the Hispanic population, is younger. All of these statistics are in stark contrast to the period between 1960 and 1980, during which the number of sixteen- to-twenty-four-year-olds nearly doubled.

Given these demographic changes, youths entering the workforce can be expected to be increasingly unqualified for the types of jobs available. In the first six months of 1987, New York Telephone gave its fifty-minute exam in basic reading and reasoning skills to 21,000 applicants for entry-level jobs. Only 16 percent passed.

New York Telephone's experience reflects an increasingly common situation in the economy today. Businesses find it more and more difficult to locate literate, entry-level young workers who have mastered basic skills. Help wanted signs can be seen everywhere. When businesses do hire entry-level workers, they are often forced to spend resources on remedial reading and writing skills. In 1982, for example, AT&T spent $6 million to train 14,000 employees in basic reading and math skills.

According to *The New York Times*, "Millions of adults whose meager schooling would not have barred them from well-paying factory jobs twenty years ago are considered unqualified today for service jobs that pay above $7 an hour." The National Alliance for Business predicts that by 1990 three out of four jobs will require some education or technical training beyond high school.

What can be done to ensure that youth will have the academic, vocational, functional, and interpersonal skills that will allow them to advance in the job market? What can be done to ensure that they make it into the job market in the first place?

Youth employment experts stress that enough information is known for action at the local, state, and national levels. Increasing the employability of youths involves a series of interventions that should take place throughout a child's life. We know that factors such as poverty, teenage pregnancy, poor academic performance, inadequate schools, school failure, and lack of parental support all contribute to a youth's potential to drop out of school and to be unemployed as an adult.

Issues and Analysis

A first issue is **the relationship of school dropout prevention to employment**. In their new book, *Dropouts in America: Enough is Known for Action*, Hahn and Danzberger emphasize that the country must develop a continuing system of prevention, remediation, and retrieval to deal with the problems of school leaving. Efforts should identify potential dropouts and at-risk children in the early grades of elementary school and continue throughout high school. Programs must be directed to the specific needs of youth, since what works for a pregnant dropout may not meet the needs of a teen who leaves school to take a job. Alternative education approaches must be implemented to reach students turned off by traditional classrooms, and continuing monitoring systems must be used by school systems to follow students throughout their entire school careers so they cannot simply disappear with no one accounting for them.

Lessons learned from program evaluations and from experience with the Comprehensive Employment and Training Act (CETA) and the Job Training Partnership Act (JTPA) offer valuable insight into the best strategies and programs that are worth replicating. Reviews of these earlier studies have been completed by Robert Lerman (an article in *Youth and Society*, 1986) and Hahn and Lerman (*What Works in Youth Employment Policy*, 1985). Their work examines programs that concentrated on raising the work capabilities of youth, (such as work experience programs, skills training, and linking work experience with school) and programs that focused on raising the demand for youth workers (such as programs to create public jobs and subsidies to private industry to stimulate jobs). The next four issues reflect these "lessons."

A second issue is **the importance of the setting**. Remedial education and skills training are very effective when delivered in residential settings. The Job Corps, originally established under the Economic Opportunity Act of 1964 and currently authorized under JTPA, is a major remedial education and skills training effort that cost the government $640 million in 1986. It provides residential services to severely educationally or economically disadvantaged sixteen-to-twenty-one-year-old youths through 106 centers in forty-two states. The Job Corps has been found to have highly beneficial impacts on participants. Those who attended Job Corps averaged $600 (15 percent) more in earnings than non-participants. It also raised the proportion completing high school and increased the proportion of young men serving in the military. An examination of Job Corps by the GAO (1986) found that youths who remained in the program for longer periods of time were more likely to have a higher hourly starting wage than youths who left before spending ninety days in the program.

The features of the Job Corps that account for its success, according to Hahn and Lerman, are its intensity of services, mix of remedial education and skills training, direct federal oversight and contracting to private management, and its residential nature allowing for concentration on employment and training.

Many youth corps and conservation corps programs have been based on the Job Corps model. The San Francisco Conservation Corps, the first municipal conservation corps in the nation, has employed and trained hundreds of youths. Mayor Diane Feinstein says that "the San Francisco Conservation Corps has done an impressive and inspiring job of making what was only a dream a vital part of our urban reality...from Chinatown to the Golden Gate Park, the Corps' efforts have added immeasurably to San Francisco's overall quality of life."

A third issue is **linking subsidized jobs with school attendance**. Providing subsidized jobs to youths on the condition that they remain in school or return to school has some positive effects on future employment levels. The Youth Incentive Entitlement Pilot Projects, which guaranteed a job to any sixteen- to-nineteen-year-old living in a poor family who had not completed high school, had more positive results. The program, which cost $2,000 per participant, raised the rate at which dropouts returned to school and increased earnings of participants.

Fourth, while summer youth employment programs are an important source of jobs for poor, minority youths, **work experience is most effective when combined with remedial education**. The largest federal youth employment and training effort, the Summer Youth Employment Program (SYEP), which provides eight-week summer jobs to low-income youth at a cost of $1,000 per participant, was found to have a slight impact on high school attendance and employment rates three months after program completion. However, SYEP was found to be effective in raising the current share of low-income youth with jobs — accounting for more than 25 percent of all summer jobs held by black teenagers. In recognition of the need for summer work to be combined with remediation, the Summer Training Education Program designed by Public/Private Ventures (P/PV) and profiled in this chapter, adds two summers of remedial education to SYEP.

Fifth, while career education programs that teach about the job market have little impact on youth employment, **job search assistance programs and pre-employment services have a positive impact**. Several federal demonstrations designed to provide pre-employment counseling, job information, and job placement were found to help youths find jobs quickly and have a positive impact on youths' short-term employment. Research results on programs such as Jobs for Delaware Graduates, which provides pre-employment services in high schools, showed that 54 percent of the youths in the program were working compared to 38 percent of the youths in a comparison group. Other programs that provide pre-employment services, job-readiness training, and job referrals, such as job clubs, were also found to have positive impacts on youth's future employment.

Sixth, when developing programs in youth employment, **it is essential to determine the types of services to offer, to whom these services should be directed, and how the programs should be administered**. Public/Private Ventures has developed a core competency strategy for which youth must develop a capacity in order to achieve stable employment. These competencies include: basic educational skills such as reading, writing, and computation; pre-employment skills, such as interviewing skills and job-finding techniques; work maturity, which includes knowledge of expected behavior in the workplace; and occupational training in specific skill areas.

In order to achieve these basic competencies, P/PV cites seven strategies that are most appropriate and should be selected based on the specific needs of individual youth: compensatory education, alternative schooling, integrated work-study, residential education and training, job-readiness training, on-the-job training, and skills training.

A community should offer a comprehensive set of services so that the needs of at-risk youth at different stages of development can be met.

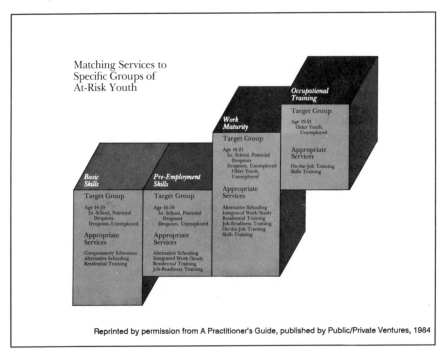

Matching Services to
Specific Groups of
At-Risk Youth

Occupational Training
Target Group
Age 19-21
Older Youth, Unemployed
Appropriate Services
On-the-Job Training
Skills Training

Work Maturity
Target Group
Age 16-21
In-School, Potential Dropouts
Dropouts, Unemployed
Older Youth, Unemployed
Appropriate Services
Alternative Schooling
Integrated Work/Study
Residential Training
Job-Readiness Training
On-the-Job Training
Skills Training

Basic Skills
Target Group
Age 14-19
In-School, Potential Dropouts
Dropouts-Unemployed
Appropriate Services
Compensatory Education
Alternative Schooling
Residential Training

Pre-Employment Skills
Target Group
Age 16-19
In-School, Potential Dropouts
Dropouts, Unemployed
Appropriate Services
Alternative Schooling
Integrated Work/Study
Residential Training
Job-Readiness Training

Reprinted by permission from A Practitioner's Guide, published by Public/Private Ventures, 1984

Seventh, experts stress that **programs should be directed at youths who are most at risk of long-term unemployment** — that is, out of school, poor, unemployed, and in their late teens and early twenties. These youths can be helped by all seven strategies, but they especially need remedial education, training, and job search and placement activities. It is important, however, that communities take a comprehensive approach to program development, which includes efforts to identify and work with potential school dropouts and younger potential dropouts and offer them services, such as alternative schools and skills training after they have mastered basic skills. It is also important to help youths in their search for jobs and give them continuing support as they search for jobs and make their initial adjustments in the workplace.

An eighth issue is **coordination and collaboration with other resources.** Many successful programs have developed public-private collaborations and partnerships that link youths with local employers as mentors, sponsors, providers of summer jobs and training programs, or adopt-a-school enhancements. For example, the Indianapolis Alliance for Jobs runs a summer youth employment program, Partners 2000, that employed more than 3,000 youth in 1986 with over 575 different employers. According to Mayor William Hudnut, "Partners 2000 captured the attention and enthusiasm of the community and offered immediate credibility to the success of the public/private partnerships while answering many of the challenges facing us."

Ninth, **quality is crucial.** Andrew Hahn, Assistant Dean at the Heller School for Advanced Studies at Brandeis University and a leading expert in the youth employment field, stresses that programs must be managed well and upgraded: "We've reached the point where it's not so much the kind of programs run as much as running them well. The burden is on all of us to get our performance up. Mayors and local level personnel need to upgrade the type of people who run second-chance programs. Technical assistance must be provided so managers of these programs can develop reputations for successful program outcomes."

Profiles

While nearly all youth employment programs have as their final goal making youth more employable, many different approaches and strategies can be used to reach that goal. The strategy of intervention should be appropriate for the child's age, educational background and basic skills level, interests, and goals. Interventions during the preschool years, such as Head Start, or during the elementary school years have been found to have positive effects on children's later success and employability, but they are not the subject of this chapter. These programs are well covered in such publications as *Children in Need: Investment Strategies for the Educationally Disadvantaged*, from the Committee for Economic Development, and *Dropouts in America: Enough is Known for Action*, from the

Institute for Educational Leadership. Both books emphasize restructuring the American school system to make it not only more relevant to youths but to affect high risk factors that lead to youths' becoming school dropouts.

The majority of youth employment programs, however, are geared to three populations: 1) youths who are in school but at risk of dropping out or at risk of future unemployability, 2) dropouts, and 3) high school graduates who lack basic skills, pre-employment skills, and/or vocational skills.

- Programs geared to in-school at-risk youths focus on keeping youths in school and linking them with the business world to better prepare them for work. These programs generally include alternative school programs, work experience programs combined with remediation, school-to-work transition programs, integrated work-study programs, and school-to-school transition programs.

- Programs geared to dropouts focus on remedial education, training, and/or pre-employment skills and for the most part are offered by private non-profit agencies operating outside the school system and receiving funding through a combination of sources, such as the Job Training Partnership Act, state departments of education or labor, major foundations, and other local sources.

- Programs that focus on high school graduates who lack pre-employment skills, basic academic skills, and/or vocational skills generally offer the same

---

INTERVENTION STRATEGIES IN YOUTH EMPLOYMENT

Preschool Years	In-School Youth	Out of School Youth
Day care Head Start	Remedial education Work experience School-to-work transition Alternative education Integrated work/study Adopt-a-school Incentives programs School/business collaboration School-to-school transition	Remedial education Pre-employment services Job readiness training Skills training On-the-job training Alternative schools Residential training

types of services as those geared to dropouts and also are generally run outside the school system.

The chart on the facing page summarizes the strategies discussed above, along with other widely used intervention strategies in youth employment. The profiles in this chapter reflect these three emphases.

Jobs for Youth/Chicago (JFY)has helped out-of-school youths get entry-level jobs and finish their educations for nearly ten years. JFY helps youths acquire pre-employment skills such as job interviewing, filling out job applications, and finding and selecting jobs. Services are available to youths for up to two years and include a learning center where they can complete work towards a GED. Counselors provide guidance and follow-up services and help clients develop career plans and set obtainable goals.

Jobs for Bay State Graduates (JBSG), Inc., in Springfield, Massachusetts, is a highly successful school-to-work transition program that operates in two Springfield high schools, as well as nineteen other Massachusetts cities and is affiliated with the Jobs for America's Graduates program that operates in twelve other states. The program offers seniors a year-long course to prepare them for, and help them find, work. Nearly all youths are placed in jobs upon graduation, and job specialists remain in touch with the youths for nine months after graduation.

In Houston, the Tenneco/Jefferson Davis Business-School Partnership is a model adopt-a-school program geared to a high school whose students are primarily Hispanic and economically and academically disadvantaged. Besides school-year services including tutoring, mentoring, volunteer work, speakers, and other activities, Tenneco also runs a subsidized summer job program for Jefferson Davis high school students.

In Mt. Clemens, Michigan, a unique alternative education program makes school relevant for dropouts by engaging them in business ventures. The Enterprise High program, currently serving more than 600 dropouts a year in Mt. Clemens and nine other Michigan cities, is expanding to Chicago and Cleveland. The program, operated by the Macomb Intermediate School District, builds its curriculum around student business ventures and simulated life situations that call for adult decision making. Students earn credit toward high school diplomas.

The Summer Training and Education Program (STEP) is a fifteen-month work experience, life skills, and remedial education demonstration operating in conjunction with local Summer Youth Employment and Training Programs in Fresno, California; Portland, Oregon; San Diego; Boston; and Seattle. Managed by Public/Private Ventures, STEP offers fourteen- and fifteen-year-old dropout-prone youths two summers of part-time SYETP work and part-time classes, plus counseling during the intervening school year. Early results show that the program is cutting summer reading losses and achieving gains in mathematics and that students are less likely to fail in school.

A forerunner in on-the-job training and skills training, Vocational Foundation Inc. (VFI) in New York City has offered services for fifty years. Since 1970, VFI has run the Joint Urban Manpower Program (JUMP) which combines classroom training and on-the-job experience for disadvantaged youths leading to guaranteed employment as draftsmen. VFI also runs training programs in the fashion industry and clerical occupations as well as literacy training, GED preparation, and job placement services.

Concluding Remarks

A community has the responsibility to educate its children, but unfortunately no community can mandate that all youths take full advantage of the opportunity. There will always be children who find school boring, irrelevant, too difficult, too easy, no match for outside interests, or unable to compete with problematic home situations. Thus, there will always be children who are at risk of dropping out, as well as millions of new dropouts each year who are at risk of chronic unemployment. There will be children who graduate but still lack basic skills or job-specific skills or goals and are not prepared to approach the work world with much promise of success.

We cannot expect this situation to improve on its own. For that matter, statistics warn us that the situation will worsen:

- One out of every four ninth graders will not graduate from high school.

- There will be fewer black male teens with work experience by the year 2000 than there are now.

- By 1990, three out of four job opportunities will require some education or technical training beyond high school while the number of illiterate adults will grow.

There is no lack of knowledge about what works in youth employment or how to turn at-risk youths into contributing citiznes. There is however, widespread unfamiliarity with youth training needs and program options. There is a great need for city halls, community agencies, schools, employment and training agencies, and businesses to work together and improve and coordinate services for youths who are most at risk of long-term unemployment. Communities should develop a comprehensive array of services — no single solution will do the job — that runs the gamut of needs of youths at risk of dropping out of school or otherwise being unqualified for jobs. Communities should direct resources to those youths most at risk of failure rather than to those easiest to serve.

Many experts agree that the country is in the process of creating a permanent societal underclass as generations become accustomed to unemployment, poverty, welfare, and crime. Ignoring this possibility will have a devastating impact not only in terms of wasted lives but on the future of American business as we are less able to compete economically. Many youth employment experts, however, are optimistic that the situation can be affected at the local level by concentrating federal, state, and local resources on the problem.

As June Bucy, executive director of the National Network of Runaway and Youth Services, says "When we reconnect young, unskilled people to the worlds of school and work, they become productive and achieving members of the community. Work with these youths is not a dead end — it's a challenge worthy of our best efforts."

A list of references and resources follows the profiles on page 106.

Programs Dealing with Youth Employment

Program Location	Population, Geography	Year Initiated	Budget	Municipal Involvement	Client Population	Services Provided	Outcome Data
Jobs for Youth Chicago IL	2,005,070 midwest	1978	$1 million	original Board of Directors	1,185 poor, out-of-school youth	pre-employment training; 2-year commitment; counseling	evaluation
Jobs for Bay State Graduates Springfield, MA	152,319	1980	$1,000 per student	local department of education funds; mayor on board of directors	200 high school seniors	school-to-work transition	evaluation
Tenneco/Jefferson Davis High School Houston, TX	1,594,090 south	1981		partnership with school	whole school	adopt-a-school year-round activities; 130 summer jobs	
Enterprise High Mt. Clemens MI	rural/suburban midwest small	1979	$4,000 per student	part of intermediate school district	45 high school dropouts	how to manage life; how to earn a living (student business venture)	longitudinal study in progress
Summer Training and Education Program Fresno CA	217,491 west	1984			300 14-15-year-olds (150 in control group, 150 in treatment group)		longitudinal study in progress
Vocational Foundation New York NY	7,071,030 east	1937	$1.4 million	city funding	1,500 out-of-school youth, many from jails and correctional facilities	on-the-job training in drafting and fashion pattern grading	

Jobs for Youth
Chicago, Illinois

Obtaining entry-level jobs and completed educations for out-of-school youths.

Contact:
John Connelly, Executive Director
Jobs for Youth/Chicago
67 East Madison Street
Room 1900
Chicago, IL 60603
312/782-2086

Jobs for Youth (JFY) in Chicago has been successfully helping poor, out-of-school youths become self-reliant, independent, and self-supporting adults for nearly ten years, by helping them prepare for, find, and keep jobs in local businesses and industry. JFY provides 16-to-21-year-old, primarily minority, youths with pre-employment training in job readiness skills, remedial education, and job placement services.

The private non-profit agency began in Chicago in 1978, based on a model originally started in New York in 1968 and replicated in Boston in 1976. The Chicago program was established with the assistance of the Boston project through a combination of funding from the Edna McConnell Clark Foundation, Mott Foundation, Department of Labor, and Ford Foundation. Representatives from Chicago Mayor Jane Byrne's office were on the original JFY Board of Directors. The program currently serves more than twice as many youths as it did when it started, and over the years has added more in-depth remedial education services and post-placement follow-up activities.

The focus of Jobs for Youth is not just on getting kids their first jobs. According to Executive Director John Connelly, "the two most critical things we do are to ensure basic literacy and teach kids that they have mobility—that they can get out of the ghetto. Many youths who come to Jobs for Youth are not exposed to a wide range of goals in life and see few possibilities or choices. It is the responsibility of JFY to help them acquire the basic skills they will need to become self-sufficient."

The program takes a comprehensive approach to working with dropouts and other young people looking for work. The staff members explain to all youngsters who enter the program that they do not intend to just get them a job and let them go. Counselors make a two-year commitment to each youth who goes through the program, and they encourage the youths to acquire any basic skills they need through the Learning Center. They help figure out life strategies so students can develop career plans.

A youth entering the program is assigned a counselor who explains the program's services. The youth is then enrolled in a three-week Pre-Employment Workshop that offers a comprehensive curriculum covering the basic prerequisites needed to get and hold any job. The curriculum covers instruction on preparing applications, finding and selecting appropriate jobs, interviewing skills, as well as a review of responsible job performance. The enrollees must report daily for the workshop, punch a time clock, and be motivated enough to complete the course.

Those who complete the workshop and are "work ready" are considered by counselors to be adequately prepared to successfully gain and hold a job. While some youths reach this point by the end of the Pre-Employment Workshop, others need substantial additional preparation. This preparation may range from counseling on appropriate dress and behavior to instruction in basic survival math or reading skills.

In addition to these services, the Learning Center at JFY offers GED preparation. Students take a diagnostic assessment test that pinpoints any deficiencies in their basic educational skills. Enrollees may choose to start and complete a GED before seeking a job or they may go on to job placement and continue to use the Learning Center over the course of the next two years. Students are taught by professional teachers and tutors and work in the Learning Center an average of three months. About 25 percent of JFY youths are found to read below the sixth grade level and need remedial work.

"Work ready" youths are referred to an Employer Services Representative by their counselors, and the representative is advised of the youth's work-related qualities and interests. The Employer Services Representative locates appropriate job openings and lines up job interviews. The Employer Representative speaks with the prospective employer after the interview and advises the counselor on the outcome. Once the youth is hired, the counselor will contact the youth every week during the first month on the job, and monthly after that, to monitor progress and resolve job-related problems as they arise. The counselor will often help the youth get a promotion or a better job.

Jobs for Youth counselors are able to secure jobs for youths that the youths themselves would not even consider applying for. One young man from Chicago's far west side who secured a job at a major Loop bank, for example, would not have considered seeking work in the Loop without JFY's assistance. In a recent videotape on the JFY program, JFY clients who are currently working in jobs they got through JFY, have this to say:

> "JFY set up interviews I wouldn't have been able to get by myself. Counselors never treated me like I was just another poor kid out of the ghetto looking for a job. They treated me like I was important and their number one priority."

> "Working has change my attitude altogether. I feel I'm worthwhile now. I love working."

> "Being employed gives me a feeling of contribution. I'm not sitting around wasting my life or my time anymore."

The JFY approach relies heavily on community support and involvement. More than 350 businesses, primarily small businesses, have been recruited to provide entry-level jobs ranging from factory work to jobs in retailing and fast foods. Nineteen business executives, many of them company chairmen or presidents, sit on the JFY board of directors. According to Liz Hersh, director of youth services, it is this link with employers that makes JFY a community effort. "Employers come to depend on us for entry-level people. They get involved in the program by providing job opportunities, and they work here as volunteers. The businesses come to rely on the kids we prepare as a service to them."

In fiscal year 1987, Jobs for Youth had 1,185 young people enrolled in its Pre-Employment Training Workshop. Out of that number, 987 (83 percent) completed the training. A total of 856 youths were served in the Learning Center through diagnostic assessments, and 150 went through Learning Center classes to work towards their GED or raise their basic skills levels. On the average, each youth received 17 hours of basic education or counseling services.

A total of 723 youths were placed in jobs at an average starting wage of $4.10 an hour. Ninety percent stayed in their original jobs at least thirty days, but the length of stay depends heavily on a youth's age and the type of job. Cost per placement averages about $765. A recent Public/Private Ventures evaluation found that JFY participants were more likely to be working than non-participants—39 percent compared to 19 percent. The evaluation also found that participants were more likely to earn more than non-participants — $4.31 per hour for JFY participants compared to $3.41 for non-participants.

The $1 million annual budget is made up of 60 percent public funds, consisting of a mix from JTPA and the U.S. Department of Education. The remainder comes from private contributions. The twenty-one full-time staff members are supplemented by 17 part-timers and 120 volunteers.

Future plans for JFY include expansion of the Learning Center so that more in-depth courses can be offered. JFY is also looking into the possibility of establishing a program where youth entrepreneurs can run their own businesses.

Jobs for Bay State Graduates, Inc.
Springfield, Massachusetts

School-to-work transition for high school seniors.

Contact:
Audrey Reed, Regional Director
JBSG
225 High Street
Holyoke, MA 01040
413/534-4573

Jobs for Bay State Graduates (JBSG) has found that preparing and motivating high school seniors to make the transition from school to work can cut youth unemployment in half. The private non-profit program is a unique education corporation affiliated with Jobs for America's Graduates, which started in Delaware in 1978 and expanded to Arizona, Michigan, New Hampshire, Vermont, Georgia, Tennessee, Ohio, Missouri, Massachusetts, Virginia, Pennsylvania and Washington.

JBSG was established in Massachusetts seven years ago and today has programs in twenty-six high schools in twenty-one Massachusetts cities: Attleboro, Cambridge, Chelsea, Chicopee, Duxbury, Everett, Fall River, Fitchburg, Haverhill, Holyoke, Leominster, New Bedford, North Adams, North Quincy, Pittsfield, Plymouth/Carver, Quincy, Shrewsbury, Springfield, Taunton, and Worcester. Each year the entire JBSG program serves approximately 1,400 students, and as of January 1986 had served a total of nearly 6,000 students.

Originally funded as one of seven national sites chosen for replication of the Jobs for Delaware's Graduates program, Jobs for Bay State Graduates was funded for a three-year demonstration period by the U.S. Department of Labor, and from the Rockefeller, Aetna, and Mott foundations. It also received grants from the Massachusetts Department of Education, Private Industry Councils, and corporations. As of June 1984, with strong support from the governor, the Joint Legislative Committee on Education, and the Massachusetts Department of Education, the legislature included a line-item appropriation in the state budget for school-to-work transition programs.

Funding flows through the Department of Education to JBSG on behalf of the twenty-one communities participating in the program. State money accounts for 80 percent of the total budget, with the remainder coming from matching grants from the cities and a small amount of private sector donations.

In seven years, the program's budget has grown from $275,000 to $1.6 million. A large share of the sites (70 percent) provide 25 percent of the local budget, which is expected after the first three years of funding.

The JBSG program is directed toward seniors who lack clearly defined career goals and skills, have no particular plans, or are not college bound or vocationally trained. Staff members identify potential students through several means: presentations to the junior class during the spring before their senior year, meetings with school guidance staffs to identify potential participants, notices on school bulletin boards and in school newspapers, and coordinating with community-based agencies such as JTPA Service Delivery Areas and Departments of Public Welfare. Lists of potential participants are drawn up and the recommended students can participate in the course if their parents' permission is received.

The program consists of classroom study in five areas, a career association, job development and placement, and follow-up. The classroom curriculum, which has been compiled in a Competency Curriculum Guide that is available for purchase, is taught by two job specialists at each site.

One of the largest JBSG programs, located in two high schools in Springfield, is serving approximately 200 high school seniors this school year. Springfield's Department of Education appropriated $21,000 to the program in 1987.

In Springfield, as in most JBSG sites, students attend JBSG classes two hours a week. They complete an average of forty classroom hours in career development, job attainment, job survival, basic skills, and leadership development. They learn how to identify occupational interests and aptitude, develop a career path, set immediate job goals, write resumes, look for jobs, handle interviews, and understand what employers expect. Students are given occupational counseling and, where appropriate, a job-shadowing experience in which they spend time with someone working in the field in which they want to work to see what the job is all about.

Two job specialists are located at the Springfield's High School of Commerce and two at Central High School. At the High School of Commerce, the specialists run four JBSG classes a day with twelve to thirty students in each class. Job specialists have an office in the high school and are generally looked upon as a resource by guidance counselors and teachers.

Each class of JBSG participants forms a career association through which they attend career workshops, sponsor presentations by local businessmen, participate in civic activities, and help each other develop leadership ability, commitment, and a positive attitude. The job specialist acts as advisor to the career association. Students spend an average of 25 hours in association activities.

The job specialists develop job referrals that have long-term career potential and match participants' interests, abilities, and aptitudes with job openings. They make at least five employer contacts a week throughout the life of the program, and they are responsible for all placement activities on behalf of their students. Job specialists attempt to have students develop relationships with potential employers by having the employers come into the classroom and talk.

All participants are followed monthly for nine months after they graduate and take jobs. The job specialists meet with employers during this time to make sure the transition is smooth and keep in close contact with the students on the job to help them deal with problems.

To encourage local private sector involvement, JBSG uses an advisory council and a board of directors made up of representatives of the private sector, education community, local government, parents of participants, and local staff. Springfield Mayor Richard Neal serves on the JBSG board of directors. The advisory council helps the program gain business community support. Businesses that participate in the program include the Bank of Boston, New England Telephone, Massachusetts Mutual Life Insurance, and Northeast Utilities.

About 70 percent of the students enrolled in JBSG in Springfield's High School of Commerce are minority students and 75 percent are female. In the four years the program has been running at the High School of Commerce, about 400 young people have gone through the program. At Central High School, a new school, about 200 students have gone through the program. Post-graduation studies show that 78 percent of the students were still working nine months after graduation, and 88 percent of the participants were working, in the military, or in college.

In an impact study on the class of 1983 and a comparison group of youths who did not participate in JBSG, Sum (1985) found that 81 percent of the JBSG participants were employed immediately following graduation, compared to 56 percent of the comparison group. The typical JBSG participant worked 43 percent more than his comparison group counterpart during the three months following graduation and earned more than twice as much.

JBSG president Lawrence Fitch reports that an important lesson learned in implementing a school-to-work transition program in a high school is to have school personnel see JBSG's work as complementary to school work. Guidance counselors and teachers may be threatened by outside personnel setting up shop in their school and it takes time for school staff members to realize they are not being replaced. Springfield job specialist Marie Pratt says that the program builds such self-esteem that school staff members quickly see it as a valuable resource.

Fitch would like to expand JBSG to twenty more sites in the next five years, depending on increased state and corporate funding. He believes the program, which costs about $1,100 per student, "gives young people a chance to grow and become self-assured and develop a sense of direction."

Information about Massachusetts' overall implementation of Jobs for America's Graduates in twenty-one cities can be obtained from Lawrence Fitch, President, Jobs for Bay State Graduates, Inc., 100 Federal Street, 17th Floor, Boston, MA 02110, 617/434-5122.

Tenneco, Inc./Jefferson Davis High School
Houston, Texas

A partnership between a business and a school.

Contact:
Carol Kemp
Community Affairs Representative
Tenneco, Inc.
P.O. Box 2511
Suite T-2430
Houston, TX 77252
713/757-2526
713/757-3930

In 1981, Tenneco, Inc., responded to a request from the Volunteers in Public Schools and the Houston Independent School District to establish a business/school partnership with a Houston school. Tenneco selected Jefferson Davis High School because it is an urban school with low achievement in a Hispanic neighborhood.

Jefferson Davis High School—70 percent Hispanic, 25 percent black and 5 percent Asian—was in trouble seven years ago when Tenneco began its program. The dropout rate approached 70 percent, barely one-fifth of the students passed proficiency tests each year, and attendance was low. The program, operated by Tenneco's Office of Community Affairs, aims at helping upgrade the quality of education at the school, reducing the dropout rate, and preparing students who are likely to drop out to assume more productive roles as workers and citizens. The goals of the program are to provide guidance, social services, and subsidized summer jobs for all academically and economically disadvantaged students who fulfill program requirements.

One unique aspect of the Tenneco business-school partnership is that it not only provides a full school year of academic activities, but it also runs a summer jobs program for more than 130 youths. The summer jobs program is managed by the local Communities in School program and provides job training and social services. Tenneco subsidizes all of the summer jobs, paying the youths $3.35 an hour for the seven-week program. Youths work four days a week and participate in enrichment activities on Friday, for which they are also paid.

Carol Kemp, Tenneco's Community Affairs Representative, recruits potential work sites and matches students with desired placements. Placements are made only at non-profit agencies, such as the Red Cross, hospitals, museums, theaters, and the mayor's office. She reports that many sites hire students part-time or after graduation, and that many students participate in the program every summer. Forty-four work sites were recruited in the 1984-1985 school year, with most of the jobs in clerical services. Ninety-seven percent of the youths complete the summer job program with a satisfactory rating from their employers, and more than 90 percent complete the assignment.

To participate in the summer jobs program, students must complete a 40-hour, year-long course in job readiness and pre-employment skills training run by Communities in School. The curriculum includes four major areas: academic preparation, personal and social development, career development, and enrichment.

The school year activities that are sponsored by Tenneco include mentoring; tutoring; speakers bureaus; attendance projects (such as a barbecue for perfect attendance); underwriting a speech tournament; math competitions; and science competitions. Tenneco sponsored a 60th anniversary celebration for the school. The company provides two four-year scholarships at graduation and also hosts a job fair for seniors and an annual awards program. Tenneco has also paid for several major school renovation and beautification projects.

The school-year activities are centered around three major activities: a career shadow day, a four-day leadership retreat, and a young volunteers program. During the career shadow day, more than 100 youths spend a full day at Tenneco paired with Tenneco employees. More than 100 Tenneco employees from departments as diverse as aviation, accounting, and legal services devote the day to showing the students what their jobs involve. The students are also given a tour of the facility and treated to lunch.

The four-day leadership retreat, held on the campus of the University of Houston, is offered every year to the youths who will be participating in the summer jobs program. The retreat provides an intensive program in communication skills, goal setting, organization, leadership, problem solving, group dynamics, and self-discovery.

Youth Employment

The young volunteers project requires participating youths to complete twenty hours of volunteer work on a different community project each year. Last year's project was a clean-up-the-beach effort.

Tenneco also sponsors several school year activities that benefit the teachers, including a teachers' retreat, teacher-of-the-month gift certificates, mini-grants (up to $250) to teachers, and paying for the principal to attend the Principal's Academy at Harvard.

Tenneco spends approximately $116,000 on the adopt-a-school project at Jefferson Davis each year, and the program has encouraged school spirit and academic achievement. The proportion of Jefferson Davis students passing proficiency tests with scores of 55 or better has increased from 19 percent in 1980 to 55 percent in 1987. Graduation levels have increased to 50 percent of an entering class. School attendance has climbed from 88 percent in 1983 to 95 percent in 1987.

Carol Kemp reports that employees are as enthusiastic as ever, but in the current economic climate, supervisors are reluctant to release employees for volunteer work. Tenneco has had to cut back its 4,000-employee staff in the past few years. Employees are allowed up to two hours a week of release time and cab vouchers to go to the school. In the future, the program may be structured so that employees give only one hour a week by increasing the mentorship program and the speakers bureau. Carol Kemp is also starting a literacy program in English as a second language; the high school students in the program will be brought to Tenneco for classes so that employees will not have to leave the building to tutor them.

Enterprise High
Mt. Clemens, Michigan

Alternative education that engages dropouts in business ventures.

Contact:
Richard Benedict, Educational Consultant
Macomb Intermediate School District
44001 Garfield Road
Mt. Clemens, MI 48043
(313) 286-8800, ext. 275

Enterprise High was established in 1979 as an experimental adult alternative school for economically disadvantaged former high school dropouts by the Macomb Intermediate School District. The school district, the regional school layer between the state and local levels, has helped establish Enterprise programs in four other Macomb County cities (Lake Shore, Romeo/Richmond, Utica, and Warren Woods) and in five cities outside the county (Fowlerville, St. Clair, Romulus, Midland, and Gibralter/Flat Rock). The Macomb Intermediate School District provides technical assistance and training through its Center for the Study of Alternatives in Education, a collaboration with Oakland University.

The Enterprise High curriculum revolves around two problems that are basic to youths who are anxious to be out on their own: how to earn a living and how to manage life. The first problem, how to earn a living, known as The Enterprise, is the focal point of the program. In The Enterprise, which takes up two and a half hours of the school day, students engage in business ventures, making products or providing services that they market themselves. The profits from all sales of products and services are divided among the students, and each student earns between $300 and $1,200.

The products or services are different at each Enterprise program, depending on the local facilities. At Mt. Clemens, students can learn woodworking, small appliance repair, and crafts. Other sites also teach graphic arts, computer repair, commercial arts, boat repair, and food preparation. Focusing on products rather than services is more rewarding for students, teachers have found. Students feel a greater sense of accomplishment when they have made something—a picnic table, for instance—that they can sell than when they deliver a service like data processing.

The second major problem in the Enterprise program—how to manage life—is dealt with through simulation and a point system. A student can earn up to ten points for each hour spent in the Enterprise program. The points translate into high school completion credits.

Assigning a simulated monetary value to the points lets the students receive a weekly "paycheck"—complete with deductions for taxes—based on the points accumulated during the week. Students "pay" for shelter, food, clothing, transportation, health care, entertainment, and other living expenses out of their "paychecks." They receive bills for these expenses, and pay their bills by check. They also take a spin on a wheel of fortune that comes up with unexpected events—and expenses—for them to cope with, including illness, car repairs, and other surprises.

Students entering the program earn points at the minimum wage; as they earn more points, their simulated wage rate increases. They quickly learn that $100 a week in take home pay is not enough to support a desirable style of life and conclude that they need more education if they want to earn more than the minimum wage.

Three other important principles form the structure of the Enterprise curriculum: basic skills practice, group problem solving, and trust.

The Enterprise venture gives teachers a way to cover basic mathematics, writing, language, and communications skills, and it gives students plenty of opportunities to practice them. Every time they work on a new product, students project expenses, write advertising, calculate paychecks, or write stories for the school newspaper. Students make decisions about products or services to offer—what to build, what to charge, how to split the profits, how to change the business plan, what the real costs of independent living are, and what the agreed-upon rules of behavior are—as a group. These and other pertinent matters are discussed in daily business meetings.

Trust is an essential part of the Enterprise program. The program stresses a caring, flexible atmosphere that is warm and affectionate. Staff members are chosen for their ability to be empathetic and accepting toward students. As Carlos, a successful Enterprise student, put it, "It blew my mind when I came here in my heavy metal outfit and these folks treated me like I was normal."

The Enterprise curriculum takes up four hours of school each day, for which students earn up to four Carnegie credits towards their high school degrees. During the two remaining periods each day, students complete other required courses, such as English or history, in classes taught by adult education teachers hired by the Enterprise program. Students receive diplomas from the local school district, rather than from the Enterprise program itself, when and if they meet the district's graduation requirements.

The Mt. Clemens Enterprise High is located in rented space in an industrial park. The warehouse-sized building is divided into classrooms and large workshops to accommodate building projects. Richard Benedict, founder of Enterprise High, stresses the need for Enterprise programs to be located away from regular high schools that may have been the scenes of negative experiences for the students.

Classes run from Monday through Thursday from 8:15 in the morning to 4:00 in the afternoon; Friday is reserved as a staff development day. The program is staffed by two teachers (English and industrial arts) and three paraprofessionals who specialize in occupational areas (woodworking, appliance repair, and crafts).

Enrollment at the Mt. Clemens Enterprise High is limited to forty-five students from sixteen- to twenty-one years old, about 20 percent of them minority students, at a cost of approximately $4,000 per student. Funds are provided through state aid from the Michigan Department of Education in the form of a $3,000 reimbursement per student for each dropout who returns to school, and from Job Training Partnership Act funds administered by the Macomb/St. Clair Employment and Training Agency. The nine other Michigan cities offering Enterprise High each enroll about fifty students and are generally located in renovated elementary schools.

Throughout the state, about 600 students are currently enrolled in Enterprise High programs. Students average two years in the program, but some complete it in one year, and others take three years. Of the students who start in the program, 80 percent successfully complete at least one year. Two thirds go to work, trade school, or college after completing the program. The program is currently studying all participants in the past five years.

Cleveland and Chicago are expecting to start Enterprise High programs by the end of 1987. (A handbook, *So You Want to Start an Enterprise Program*, is available at a nominal cost.)

Youth Employment

Richard Benedict attributes the program's success to the staff's caring attitude and the pride instilled in students by the ownership they feel in the products they develop and the services they offer. He has seen students who entered the program with an "us against them" attitude become, in just a few months, warm and professional when selling their products to the public.

The most difficult part of starting an Enterprise program, according to Benedict, is motivating schools and cities to devote resources to working with high school dropouts. But, he says, the financial rewards alone are worth it for a community. The investment of $4,000 in successfully training one student for one year earns a 34 percent return on investment annually compared to the costs that might be incurred if the students end up on public assistance or in jail.

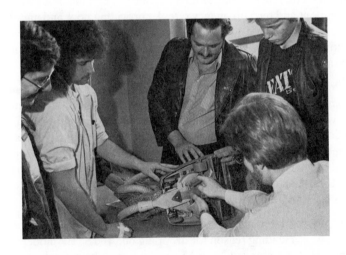

Learning small appliance repair can mean big steps toward independent living for students at Enterprise High in Mt. Clemens, Michigan. The unique program uses student business ventures to teach skills for jobs—and skills for living. Used with permission.

Summer Training and Education Program
Fresno, California

Combining remedial education with summer jobs.

Contact:
Linda Wood
Youth Services Coordinator
Fresno Private Industry Council
1025 N. Abbey Street
Fresno, CA 93701
(209) 233-4500

The Summer Training and Education Program (STEP) increases basic skills and lowers dropout and teen pregnancy rates by providing poor and under-performing youths with remedial education, life skills, and work experience during two consecutive and intensive summer programs, augmented by support and personal contact during the intervening school year.

Public/Private Ventures (P/PV), a non-profit Philadelphia research and program development organization, started STEP as a national four-year demonstration in 1984. Four other cities — San Diego, Seattle, Boston, and Portland, Oregon — are participating. Aware that learning slows, stops, or even regresses during the summer, particularly for disadvantaged youths, P/PV uses the federal summer youth employment program to improve reading and math skills of participants, increase the graduation rate, and reduce the incidence of teen parenthood among disadvantaged youths who are doing poorly in school.

Because summer learning is a critical factor in education, and poor academic performance is a leading reason for dropping out, the STEP model is geared to economically disadvantaged 14 to 15 year olds who have reading and/or math skills well below their grade level and/or had been left back at least once in school.

In Fresno, as in the other STEP sites, 300 youths are recruited each year. Half are assigned to a treatment group and half to a control group; the progress of both groups will be followed until 1993, so the effectiveness of the program can be judged. Youths in the control group work full-time on JTPA Summer Youth Employment and Training Program (SYETP) jobs. Youths in the treatment group participate in the STEP program for fifteen months. During each of the two summers, they take ninety hours of remedial programs and eighteen hours of life skills and opportunities instruction and spend at least eighty hours at part-time work on SYETP jobs. During the school year, the youths participate in individual counseling and group activities. Participants are paid the minimum wage five days a week for six to eight weeks during the summer.

So far, two cohorts have completed the program; the third is in the middle of the school year and will complete the program in the summer of 1988. The Fresno Private Industry Council, the lead agency for STEP's operational and fiscal management, contracts with the Economic Opportunity Commission for outreach, recruitment, and work site development for STEP youth. Remedial programs are the responsibility of the Fresno Unified School District.

Students are selected from all over Fresno to participate in the STEP program. The remedial and life skills classes are held at the Tehipite Middle School, centrally located near downtown Fresno. During the summer, STEP classes are held five mornings a week. Youths in the treatment group work two-and-a-half to four hours each afternoon at jobs in schools, parks, government offices, and private businesses throughout the city. Sixteen remedial education teachers are involved in the STEP program, as well as four life skills teachers and one additional instructional leader who directs the classroom part of the program. P/PV provides a site coordinator who gives technical assistance and monitoring assistance.

The STEP curriculum, called "Practical Academics," is skills-based, individualized, and structured around learning modules that relate reading and mathematics to the STEP program and to the youths' own life experiences, job skills, and life skills. Each module contains three elements: the presentation of a theme or topic, assignments of activities and projects that require reading and math skills for successful completion, and activities that reinforce those skills. Job skills modules include such topics as getting and handling jobs and adjusting to the world of work. The life skills modules include such topics as substance abuse, decisions, and self-identity. Instruction also involves computer-assisted instruction and silent, sustained reading.

During the school year, STEP offers participants sessions with a personal mentor or counselor at least twice a month and regular group and social activities. The six counselors in Fresno, all graduate students, are assigned a caseload of twenty-five to thirty students. The mentoring provides individual attention to participants and helps the youths deal with academic or personal problems that may make school difficult. The counselors meet with the students individually and run group events, such as trips to the university campus or local businesses. Counselors run at least four career-focused events a year. They also run a number of social events, such as banquets for students, teachers, and parents, that are rewards for improved attendance and grades. The counselors also make referrals to social service or tutoring programs as needed.

The STEP participants who joined the Fresno program in the summer of 1986 were 54 percent male, 46 percent female; 44 percent Hispanic, 30 percent black, and 14 percent Asian; 57 percent were fourteen years old when they entered the program, and 43 percent were fifteen; 35 percent had been held back in school.

Research on the two total cohorts of STEP participants showed that the program is having positive results, more so with the second group than with the first, because the remedial curriculum was refined in the second year. In reading, STEP participants had very little learning loss, outscoring control group youths by six-tenths of a grade. In math, they not only overcame all learning losses but gained on the control group, ending the summer eight-tenths of a grade ahead. The results were consistent at all sites and for all racial and ethnic groups and both sexes. STEP participants were better informed about contraception, and there was a measurable effect on their behavior: those who were sexually active were 53 percent more likely to use contraceptives than were youths in the control group.

Funding for the development and startup of STEP was provided by $3 million in grants from the Ford Foundation. Continuing funding comes from the Ford Foundation, the Department of Labor, The Robert Wood Johnson Foundation, W.T. Grant Foundation, The Edna McConnell Clark Foundation, the William and Flora Hewlett Foundation, the Department of Health and Human Services, Lilly Endowment, the Ahmanson Foundation, Aetna Life and Casualty Foundation, and the James C. Penney Foundation.

Two summers of STEP and one year of school-year support costs $1,600 in addition to the per-enrollee costs of SYETP.

Public/Private Ventures will follow all STEP treatment and control youths until 1993, six months after the scheduled graduation date for the third cohort of students. Telephone and in-person surveys will be used to track the effect of STEP in terms of early labor market experience, dropout rates, teenage parenting, and other data. Currently, P/PV is developing a formal replication strategy. Since the 1986 JTPA amendments mandate that the Summer Youth Employment and Training Program include remedial education beginning in 1987, P/PV's work on the STEP program is particularly relevant. Service Delivery Areas will be required to assess the reading and math skills of SYTEP participants to determine whether they need remedial education. Service Delivery Areas should therefore be particularly interested in examining STEP.

For further information on implementation of the national STEP demonstration, in the other four cities, contact Natalie Jaffe, Director of Communications, Public/Private Ventures, 399 Market Street, Philadelphia, PA 19106; 215/592-9099

Vocational Foundation, Inc.
New York, New York

On-the-job training and skills training for dropouts.

Contact:
 Rebecca Taylor, Executive Director
 Vocational Foundation, Inc.
 902 Broadway
 New York, N.Y. 10010
 212/777-0700

On-the-job training programs and on-the-job training combined with classroom training give unskilled teenagers the edge they need to gain access to employment opportunities that have career development potential. Research has shown that the longer the training, the greater the gains in future earnings and the more likely is success in continued advancement in the work world.

Established in 1937 to find jobs for young people who had spent time in jail or correctional facilities, Vocational Foundation, Inc. (VFI) today still takes about 30 percent of its clients from jails and correctional facilities. About half of all the youths who come to VFI are referred by courts, agencies, schools, or social service agencies, and half hear about VFI services by word of mouth.

VFI's goal is to bring inner-city youths into the adult world of jobs and families. They see more than 1,500 youth every year, most of them high school dropouts. VFI, in fact, does not work with youths who are still in school. Youths entering VFI are tested to gauge their reading and math abilities. They talk with counselors about their goals and interests and then determine which of VFI's programs to enter. Programs include:

- a literacy program that provides a half-day of basic skills education and a half-day of part-time employment five days a week over a four-month period leading to full-time jobs or other types of training programs;

- basic skills/GED completion;

- job placement services for entry-level jobs;

- on-the-job training programs for entry-level jobs; and

- classroom training combined with salaried on-the-job training in specific industries.

VFI also offers special services for ex-offenders and a new teen fathers program that helps young fathers assume financial and personal responsibility for their children. VFI will tailor its services into combinations that meet an individual youth's needs—from part-time employment to job counseling, to classes after work. They firmly believe that once working, a client is more likely to accept educational programs.

The most established and well-known of VFI's on-the-job training programs is the drafting and construction inspection program. The Joint Urban Manpower Program, or JUMP, has been preparing about fifty youths a year for guaranteed jobs as junior draftsmen or construction inspectors since 1970. The program, a joint effort between New York City's seven architectural and engineering societies and VFI, has trained nearly 430 youths. The training program runs for five months and is funded by the Department of Transportation (DOT). More than sixty architectural and engineering firms guarantee placements for every student in the program. Different firms are involved from year to year, depending on the size of each year's class. In 1986, for example, twenty-four firms provided guaranteed jobs for the fifty trainees in the program.

During the first five months, trainees spend half a day in the VFI classroom, learning drafting skills from an in-house teacher. The only requirement for the trainees is that they have attained at least seventh grade reading or math scores and that they be mature enough to stick with the year-long program. Afternoons are spent on the job at the firms where they will eventually work. The trainees are paid $5.00 an hour for the entire day, and earn about $10,000 a year while in training. After they receive certificates of completion from VFI, the trainees spend the next six months working full time. They receive personal attention from teachers and supervisors, and they are encouraged to earn their GEDs.

The JUMP directors change the curriculum to follow job trends. During years when architecture is in a slump, for example, the program emphasizes training aimed toward civil engineering. The firms guaranteeing jobs pay the trainees' salaries and pay VFI for its services. If the firms have a DOT contract, they are reimbursed by DOT; if not, they are reimbursed through the Private Industry Council (PIC). The PIC will reimburse 100 percent for classroom time and 50 percent for on-the-job training time. The average cost for training in the JUMP program is $4,000, considerably higher than VFI's other on-the-job training programs. But a job retention study shows that after seven years, 72 percent of JUMP trainees were still with the firms in which they were placed.

VFI's second industry-specific on-the-job training program is its fashion industry pattern grading program, developed jointly with the Fashion Institute of Technology, a community college of the State University of New York. The six-month training program operates much like the drafting program. An employer consortium of pattern service companies and manufacturers is recruited before the start of each training cycle. The companies agree to hire trainees and provide afternoon on-the-job training for 20 hours a week for 26 weeks; the students attend classes in the morning. The participants are paid $4.50 an hour, and the employers cover half of the trainees' wages. The PIC reimburses employers for 50 percent of the on-the-job training wages and 100 percent of the classroom hours. The total trainee costs are $2,250. The classroom training is held at the Fashion Institute of Technology, four mornings a week, for a total of 240 hours. Students learn all aspects of pattern grading for women's, misses, and children's garments. A half-day of remedial math instruction is provided by VFI. Thirty-four youths completed the program in 1986. Within two years on the job, trainees are able to earn $6 to $8 an hour, and $10 an hour after three years.

The clerk-typist training program is taught at VFI for four months, after which the trainees are placed in jobs. Youths are reimbursed $30 a week through JTPA funds, but they can earn $175 to $235 a week after training. VFI will also contact youths after placement to help them move up to better jobs.

VFI has an annual budget of more than $1.4 million, and a staff of 29 full-time employees. Seventy percent of VFI's funds come from government, including the New York City Department of Employment, Youth Bureau, Mayor's Office of Criminal Justice, the Job Training Partnership Act, and the Department of Transportation. The remaining 30 percent comes from private foundations, corporations, and donations.

Executive Director Rebecca Taylor stresses that the most difficult aspect of a training program is to develop commitments from employers to hire young people and to develop the industry contacts. She says it is important to use people who have a good knowledge of the companies in the industry. But she remains committed to on-the-job training because it has demonstrated long-term benefits. "Youths who complete our program have higher salaries and stay with the same companies for long periods of time. They are getting a two-for-one deal—job specific training and basic skills—that provides the motivation for them to keep on progressing."

References

Committee for Economic Development. 1987. *Children in Need. Investment Strategies for the Educationally Disadvantaged*. New York and Washington, D.C.

de Lone, R. and Long, M. 1983. *What do you Know About Youth Unemployment?* Philadelphia: Public/Private Ventures.

Farkas, G., R. Olsen, E.W. Stromsdorfer, L.C. Sharpe, F. Skidmore, D.A. Smith, and S. Merrill. 1984. *Post-Program Impacts of the Youth Incentive Entitlement Projects*. New York: Manpower Demonstration Research Corp.

Hahn, A. and Lerman, R. 1985. *What Works in Youth Employment Policy?* Washington, D.C.: National Planning Association.

Hahn, A. and Danzberger, J. with Bernard Lefkowitz. 1987. *Dropouts in America: Enough is Known for Action*. Washington, D.C.: Institute for Educational Leadership.

Lefkowitz, B. 1982. *Jobs for Youth: What We Have Learned*. New York: Edna McConnell Clark Foundation.

Lerman, R. "Unemployment Among Low-Income and Black Youth," *Youth and Society*, Vol. 17 No. 3, March 1986, pp. 237-266.

Mallar, C., Kerachsky, S. and Thornton, C.V. 1982. *Evaluation of the Economic Impact of the Job Corps Program* (Third Follow-up Report). Princeton, N.J.: Mathematica Policy Research, Inc.

McCarthy, W. with D. Jones, R. Penne, and L. Watkins. 1985. *Reducing Urban Unemployment*. Washington, D.C.: National League of Cities.

National Alliance of Business. 1986. *Employment Policies: Looking to the Year 2000*. Washington, D.C.

National Foundation for the Improvement of Education. 1987. *A Blueprint for Success. Community Mobilization for Dropout Prevention*. Washington, D.C.

Pressman, H. 1981. *Linking School and Work*. Washington, D.C.: Youthwork, Inc.

Public/Private Ventures. 1984. *A Practitioner's Guide. Strategies, Programs, and Resources for Youth Employability Development*. Philadelphia, Pa.: Author.

Sadd, S., Kotkin, M. and Friedman, S. 1983. *Alternative Youth Employment Strategies Project*. New York: Vera Institute of Justice.

Slobig, F. and George, C. 1983. *A Policy Blueprint for Community Service and Youth Employment*. Washington, D.C.: Roosevelt Centennial Youth Project.

Sklar, Morton. *Making Effective Youth Programming Choices Under JTPA*. Washington, D.C.: National Association of Counties, March 1986.

Sum, Andrew. 1982. "A Review of the Impact of Pre-employment Programs on Disadvantaged Youth." Brandeis University, Center for Human Resources, Waltham, (MA).

Taggart, R. 1981. *Fisherman's Guide: An Assessment of Training and Remediation Strategies.* Kalamazoo, (MI).: Upjohn Institute.

Taggart, R. 1980. "The Youth Employment Problem: A Sequential and Development Perspective." *A Review of Youth Employment Problems, Programs and Policies.* Vol. 1. Washington, D.C.: The Vice-President's Task Force on Youth Employment.

U.S. General Accounting Office. 1980. *CETA Demonstration Provides Lessons on Implementing Youth Programs.* Washington, D.C..

U.S. General Accounting Office. 1986. *Dropouts: The Extent and Nature of the Problem.* Washington, D.C.

U.S. General Accounting Office. 1986. *Job Corps. Its Costs, Employment Outcomes, and Service to the Public.* Washington, D.C.

U.S. General Accounting Office. 1986. *Labor Market Problems of Teenagers Result Largely from Doing Poorly in School.* Washington, D.C.

U.S. General Accounting Office. 1987 *School Dropouts. Survey of Local Programs.* Washington, D.C.: Author.

Resources

Other programs relating to alternative education and dropout prevention include:

Peninsula Academies Model Programs
Sequoia Union High School District
480 James Avenue
Redwood City, Calif. 95062
415/369-1411
Marilyn Raby, Special Programs Coordinator

School to Work Action Program (SWAP)
Colorado Alliance of Business
600 Grant Street
Suite 204
Denver, Colo. 80203
303/832-9791
Susan Klein, Training Program Manager

Other programs providing summer work experience and remediation include:

Partners 2000
Indianapolis Alliance for Jobs, Inc.
32 East Washington Street
Indianapolis, Ind. 46204
317/632-2850
Alicia Chadwick,
Vice-President of Marketing

Futures
101 West 24th Street
Baltimore, Md. 21218
301/396-7510
Carol Wheeler, Barbara Sembly

Other programs providing skills training based on the Job Corps model include:

San Francisco Conservation Corps
Building 111
Fort Mason
San Francisco, Calif. 94123
415/928-7322
Richard Woo,
Program Director

City Volunteer Corps
842 Broadway
New York, N.Y. 10003
212/475-6444
Suzanne Goldsmith,
Public Affairs Officer

Other programs relating to school-to-work or school-to-school transition include:

Job Readiness Training
MDC, Inc.
1717 Legion Road
P.O. Box 2226
Chapel Hill, N.C. 27514
919/968-4531
Carol Lincoln

Career Beginnings Program
Heller Graduate School
Brandeis University
Waltham, Mass. 02254
617/343-3770
800/343-4705 (toll free)
Erik P. Butler, Program Codirector

Other programs providing skills training and services for dropouts include:

JOBSTART
Manpower Development Research Corp. (MDRC)
3 Park Avenue
New York, N.Y. 10016
212/532-3200
Robert Ivry, Senior Vice-President

70001 Ltd.
600 Maryland Avenue SW
West Wing
Suite 300
Washington, D.C. 20024
202/484-0103
Steve Hines, Director of Communications

Organizations

National Youth Employment Coalition
Room 1111
1501 Broadway
New York, N.Y. 10036
212/840-1801
Donald Mathis, Executive Director

Youth Service America
810 18th Street NW
Suite 705
Washington, D.C. 20006
202/783-8855
Frank Slobig, Executive Director

Publications

*A Practitioner's Guide.
Stratgies, Programs, and Resources
for Youth Employability*
Public/Private Ventures
399 Market Street
Philadelphia, PA 19106
215/592-9099

*Dropouts in America. Enough is Known
for Action*
Institute for Educational Leadership
1001 Connecticut Avenue NW
Washington, DC 20036
202/822-8405

The Safe Place logo identifies Louisville stores, shops, fast food restaurants, and other places where homeless or runaway youths can find help. This logo is a registered service mark of the YMCA of Greater Louisville; it can be used only with their express permission.

Chapter V

Child and Family Homelessness
by Carol A. Morrow

> *"All the apartments were too expensive, or they would say 'no children'.... So, we lived in our Ford, all five of us, parking on a different street every night. It was so horrible living in the streets, freezing in the car. I could not bear to let the children live in the car anymore so I did the only thing I could do. I brought them to the Department of Youth and Family Services. It broke my heart...I felt like a terrible mother. DYFS put my kids in foster homes and split them up. It was over three weeks before they told me where my kids were. I wanted to kill myself. All I did since my children were away from me was cry, because I missed them so much. It was like living in a nightmare. NOTHING is worse than being homeless."*
>
> *Rebecca Ayres in testimony before a Congressional hearing,*
> *February 24, 1987*

The harsh reality of homelessness that faces hundreds of thousands of American families and children is reflected in this true story of one family's agonizing experience. It happened suddenly. The husband lost his job; family savings dwindled; the utilities were shut off; and the family was evicted. There were no relatives to turn to, and friends could not help. There was no place to go. They became homeless.

What's the end of the story? In this particular case, there is a happy ending. With the help of public and private resources, the family was reunited in an affordable apartment, and the husband found new employment. But for large numbers of homeless families and children, there has yet to be a happy ending.

Background

Homeless children and families, one third of the homeless population, have emerged in the 1980's as one of the most formidable problems confronting American society. Although images of skid row alcoholics and "bag ladies" still dominate the public perception of homelessness, it is increasingly clear that America's homeless are uniform neither in characteristics nor needs. They include the old and the young, men and women, families and children, whites and minorities, the physically disabled and the mentally ill, veterans and civilians, and workers and the unemployed.

The fastest growing segment of the homeless population is made up of families and children. In the last two years, the increase has ranged from 30 percent to 100 percent, depending on locale. A National League of Cities survey revealed that homelessness is a severe problem in more than half of the U.S. cities surveyed. A 1987 study by the U.S. Conference of Mayors found that 95 percent of Norfolk, Virginia's homeless population was made up of families (one or two adults with at least one dependent child); in New York City, families made up 63 percent of the homeless population, and in Portland, Oregon, 52 percent. Increases in the number of homeless families have been reported by urban, suburban, and rural communities across the nation. Among the cities surveyed by the U.S. Conference of Mayors, more than 90 percent expected continued increases in 1988. If this projection becomes reality, as many as one-quarter million families and one-half million children will be homeless at one time or another, confirming similar estimates reported by the National Coalition for the Homeless in the March 1987 issue of *Safety Network*.

One-third of these homeless families are headed by two parents, with one or both parents unemployed. The remaining two-thirds are families with single parents, primarily headed by females. With the trends toward single parenting and the feminization of poverty continuing, the number of one-parent homeless families seems likely to rise.

Along with sharp increases in the number of homeless families with children, the number of children who are homeless on their own has risen dramatically. These children are given a variety of labels, including "runaways," "throwaways," "delinquents," and "children in child welfare placements without homes to return to." Estimating their numbers accurately is complicated by their different labels and separate service systems. In 1986, more than 75,000 runaway children were served by youth shelters (U.S. Department of Health and Human Services, March 1987). Annually, more than 60,000 youngsters leave foster care or public institutions; many of them leave public care without the skills to live independently.

Homelessness has been identified as a primary reason for placing children in the care of the public child welfare system. Although single men constitute more than 50 percent of the homeless, the percentage of homeless women has steadily increased. Approximately 15 percent of the homeless are single women, and at least one-third of these women have children. The children are in temporary living arrangements with friends or relatives or are in public care. As reported by the Association for Children of New Jersey in a hearing before the U.S. House of Representatives Select Committee on Children, Youth, and Families, as many as 40 percent of New Jersey foster care placements in 1985 were children who had been placed in foster care because their families could not locate adequate housing and were therefore homeless.

Conservative estimates suggest that 90,000 families and more than 200,000 children will be homeless in 1987. More liberal estimates predict that 250,000 families and as many as 600,000 children will become homeless in 1987 (*Safety Network*, March 1987). And the number of homeless children, just like the number of homeless families, is expected to grow. For instance, neither the conservative nor the liberal estimates include families and children who are living on the brink of homelessness.

The debate over the true number of homeless Americans, begun in the early 1980s, continues in 1987. Early estimates were extremely speculative, reflecting confusion about how to define and accurately count the homeless, severe understaffing in shelters, and rudimentary data collection systems. The debate intensified in 1984 when the federal *Report to the Secretary on the Homeless and Emergency Shelters* suggested that the total number of homeless in the United States was between 250,000 to 350,000. Estimates from provider and advocacy sources, however, were significantly higher. The Community for Creative Non-Violence in D.C. contended that more than three million Americans were homeless. The National Coalition for the Homeless offered evidence suggesting more than two million homeless—1 percent of the total U.S. population.

Although there is now a wider consensus regarding definitions of homeless populations, and data collection and research have improved with tracking systems and information networking, the core of the debate, overcounting versus undercounting, still remains. Overcounting has been alleviated somewhat by better communication and accountability within the service community. Undercounting occurs because the lack of adequate resources means that unknown numbers of the homeless are not recorded by the shelter or service system. These homeless individuals, families, and children are hidden—hidden in the streets, in abandoned houses, in cars, and in doubled or tripled living arrangements. These individuals are actually homeless, intermittently homeless, or at imminent risk of becoming homeless. Regardless of the precise number, one point is clear: the numbers are large and merit our attention to causes, effects, and solutions.

The causes of child and family homelessness are intricate and interwoven. Among them are continuing unemployment, eroding family wages, inadequate and unaffordable housing stock, and decreased federal support across a range of housing, employment, and social services. The homeless are families and individuals who have long lived on the brink of poverty and have been unable to cope with the negative economic and social trends of the recent decade. They have been pushed into the ultimate stage of poverty: homelessness.

The economy is a pivotal factor. The economic instability of the 1970s and 1980s generated high levels of unemployment and inflation. The cost of living rose dramatically, wages stagnated, and jobs for low-skilled workers decreased. The result has been a significant increase in the number of poor. By 1986, more than 32 million Americans were poor. More than 40 percent of these poor are children. Two thirds of the poor are single parent families struggling to survive on fixed or minimal incomes. In 1987, many of these poor became America's homeless families and children.

Economic growth by itself will not resolve homelessness. Nationwide, one of every five homeless persons works, but their meager earnings fail to stave off homelessness, according to the Democratic Study Group. Other major social and economic efforts are needed to repair the human damage and give homeless families and individuals opportunities to reconstruct productive futures.

A second primary cause of homelessness is the lack of affordable housing, as seen in the results of a recent NLC survey, *A Time to Build Up*. More than 500,000 low-income housing units are eliminated annually through conversion, gentrification, abandonment, or demolition (*Safety Network*, May 1987). More than 12 million poor families compete for publicly subsidized housing, which has always fallen far short of the need. So far in the 1980s, federal funding of low-income housing programs has fallen by 60 percent.

More than 5.5 million individuals and families live in overcrowded or substandard facilities (National Institute of Building Sciences, 1987). The structures pose an assortment of constant threats to health and safety, including lead paint, asbestos, inadequate plumbing, unsafe wiring, rotting foundations, and dangerous heating and cooking utilities. Unknown numbers of poor families share living arrangements, multiplying the unsafe conditions. These families cannot locate affordable housing. Such units will become even scarcer in the future. In the decade ahead, the number of low-income households needing such units will increase to more than 13 million. At the same time, the supply of affordable units will drop to less than 5 million. The result is easily predictable: more, rather than less, homeless households in the future.

A third factor is that the New Federalism of the 1980s reduces federal funds and resources and challenges states and localities to take control and responsibility for programs for the disadvantaged. Federal funds for critical public programs — including child welfare, health and nutrition services, legal aid, education and training, counseling, and emergency assistance — have been reduced by 10 percent to 60 percent. State and local governments have been overwhelmed with these challenges, and not all of them have been able to meet them successfully.

Both the short-term and long-term effects of homelessness are devastating.

A sixteen-year-old boy in Salt Lake City, Utah, quoted in the *Washington Post* on June 21, 1987, said, "I like to go off where no one can find me and just ponder different things I've been through, such as being in a shelter, being looked upon as someone who'll never have anything in life. It makes you feel like you'll just explode."

A shelter counselor in Los Angeles, California, reported in the U.S. Conference of Mayors survey: "A homeless family with two young children lived in the back seat of a car for long periods before finally finding shelter. In the new shelter, the children were unable to play on the floor. It turned out that in order to play they had to first find a couch or a large chair which possessed the familiar configuration of a car's back seat."

An administrator of a transitional facility in the Bronx, New York: "They're shell-shocked...City shelters today are a war zone." (*Cathedral*, March 1987)

Homelessness is an intensely damaging experience that may affect individuals physically, emotionally, psychologically, and spiritually. Problems accompanying homelessness defy easy division into cause and effect. The list of problems is extensive: drug or alcohol abuse; family violence; family breakdown; foster placement; runaways; incarceration of children and adults; suicide; truancy; illiteracy; illegitimacy; health and mental health problems; and multigenerational poverty.

The consequences of homelessness for children cut across physical, emotional, intellectual, and social realms. Shelters are often located in dangerous neighborhoods, where drugs, prostitution, and violence are common. Lead paint and asbestos contamination have been found in some homeless facilities. In one New York hotel used as a family shelter, more than 1,000 health and safety violations were cited. A twelve-year-old girl described the hotel this way:

> "I don't like the hotel because there is a lot of trouble there. Many things happen that make me afraid. I don't go down in the street to play....I play in the hallways. Sometimes you can find needles and other things that drugs come in. This Saturday my friend the security guard was killed on my floor." (U.S. House of Representatives, Select Committee on Children, Youth, and Families, February 24, 1987, p.10.)

Homeless shelters often lack cooking and refrigeration facilities. Homeless infants and children can suffer staph infections, gastroenteritis, and related illnesses because of unsanitary conditions or spoiled food. James Wright's evaluation of health care among the homeless in 19 cities shows that the rate of chronic health problems among homeless children is twice that of the general child population.

The impact of homelessness on children's development is marked. Homeless children exhibit developmental delays — they don't walk, sit up, or talk on time. They experience developmental regression — older children wet the bed, children who have been toilet-trained go back to diapers, and children who could walk return to crawling (McChesney, 1986).

Children's mental health is also significantly affected. Whether mental illness is the cause or product of homelessness, more than one-third of all homeless mothers and as many as two-thirds of all homeless children exhibit mental health problems requiring psychiatric services (Bassuk, 1986). The Democratic Study

Child and Family Homelessness

Group estimates that at least one third of the total homeless population suffers from mental illness or mental health problems. Half of the children in Massachusetts shelters exhibited intense stress, anxiety, and depression. Stress and anxiety symptoms included excessive crying, clinging to parents, withdrawal, nightmares, and physiological complaints. One-quarter of the children needed psychiatric treatment. The effects on children's mental health are grim: a three-month-old infant failing to thrive; a nine-year-old saying he wanted to kill himself; a ten-year-old pulling out three teeth because he was worried (Bassuk, 1986).

Older homeless children also suffer. June Bucy, the Director of the National Network of Runaway and Youth Services summarizes some of the problems: "Homeless youth have significant health problems, including poor nutrition, drug and alcohol abuse, and sexually transmitted diseases, with extremely high incidence of AIDS-type infections." Extreme depression is common among homeless youth. More than 40 percent of all runaway and homeless youth have exhibited suicidal impulses (Rothram, 1985).

Homelessness has major effects on educational development. At a St. Louis shelter, 80 percent of the children showed significant language deprivation, a key predictor of school success (Whitman, 1987). In a shelter school in Salt Lake City, both young and older children evidenced short attention spans, passive or aggressive behavior, and communication problems. In the study of Massachusetts shelter children, the following data emerged: 43 percent of the children had repeated grades; 21 percent of the children were failing or performing below average; and 25 percent required special classes.

Maza and Hall, in a recent national study, found that 43 percent of school-age homeless children were not attending school. There are many barriers to these children's access to educational facilities — both at schools near where their shelters are located because of lack of a permanent address, and at schools in their former neighborhoods because they no longer reside there or they lack transportation. The dilemma is sketched by Helen Adams, an Alabama shelter director: "I begged the local schools to take the children, but they said they didn't have the money and the children weren't legal residents."

The impacts of homelessness on families are equally painful. The stress of homelessness debilitates marital and family relationships. The stress of shelter living distorts relationships between parents and children, causing both intense dependency and the breakdown of natural bonds between parents and children.

Individuals, children, and families may or may not recover from homelessness. Homelessness may temporarily or permanently impair the ability of children and adults to grow and develop as stable and productive citizens. Today's homeless children may become tomorrow's despondent and dependent adults. Today's homeless families and children may be on welfare for a generation. In the words of the executive director of the National Coalition for the Homeless, "We are throwing away a whole generation when we allow children to grow up homeless."

Issues and Analysis

Addressing homelessness requires careful consideration of several issues.

First, a significantly **increased supply of adequate and affordable housing** is the most critical ingredient in effective services for homeless families and children. Most simply defined, homelessness is lack of a home. Families become and remain homeless because they cannot find housing. Low-income families confronted with spiraling rents and doubled and tripled living arrangements have been catapulted into homelessness. To obtain low-cost or subsidized housing, families wait on lists for as long as fifteen years — an entire childhood. Homeless families and children need new or alternative housing models, such as: modules or mobile units; congregate and shared housing; scattered-site low-income units; family hotels and single-room-occupancy structures; family partnerships and matching; and public housing projects. Programs serving homeless families and children must link closely with these permanent housing resources.

Second, **employment services are fundamental** to helping homeless parents and older homeless youth. Homeless youths need comprehensive job services to prepare them for meaningful employment. Both single-parent and two-parent households need help to find the education, training, and support services to assure productive futures. Two-thirds of all homeless families are headed by young, single females who often lack the knowledge and skills to locate adequate employment and may encounter wage or sex discrimination as they pursue employment. Legal services may be needed to challenge employment systems or to pursue child support payments.

Third, **public assistance is not the long-term answer**, but it can help homeless families bridge the crisis. Current programs, however, are woefully inadequate. Grant amounts assure, rather than alleviate, dependency. Assistance is unavailable to two-parent families in half of the states. Some localities deny access based on lack of a permanent residence. Extensive delays in processing often exacerbate family crises. Medical assistance, cited as a critical concern of homeless parents for their children, may not be available. Few public programs offer resources to prevent homelessness. For example, lack of resources to stave off evictions or utility cutoffs are primary factors in family homelessness.

Fourth, if homelessness among American children and families is to be reduced, the design of future **interventions must be more comprehensive**. The literature is emphatic: shelter and minimum services fail to solve the problems. Shelter may be the most immediate need, but these homeless need more than a place to sleep for a night. The extensive spectrum of needs includes: transitional and permanent housing; employment; income assistance; education; medical care; social and mental health services; child care; legal aid; and, services for special populations, e.g., runaways and battered women.

Fifth, **direct services to homeless children need to be provided** rather than solely relying on indirect services provided as part of stabilizing families through parent services. Direct services for children in shelters have been minimal, nonexistent or crisis-oriented. Shelter children often lack schooling, counseling, structured child care and other specialized children's programs.

Sixth, **interim, or shelter, facilities for homeless children and families must also be significantly expanded**. The supply of shelter beds for all homeless groups has fallen far short of the need. The lack of resources for homeless families and children is even more severe. Nationwide, one family in three is turned away because of lack of shelter space. In two-thirds of the cities surveyed by the U.S. Conference of Mayors, families must break up in order to be accommodated. Older male children have been housed in shelters that serve only adult males. In the most extreme cases, children have been placed in foster homes while their parents have remained homeless.

Seventh, **homeless families desperately need transitional facilities** – where the dual goal is to provide longer-term, non-crisis oriented shelter and to provide help in solving the long-term problem permanently. But transitional programs are even scarcer than family shelters. The oldest transitional models are those designed to house persons who are victims of domestic violence. Each year approximately half a million women and their children become homeless because of domestic violence. The Women's Institute for Housing and Economic Development reports that half of these families are unable to locate transitional programs. Some of these women and children return to abusive homes as the only alternative to continued homelessness. The lack of transitional resources strains shelters as well as homeless families. It is not unusual for families to stay for months in emergency shelters where stays are officially limited to a month or less. Other families cannot be served because sheltered families cannot find the next place to go. Families are released back to the streets or cycled from shelter to shelter and back again.

Eighth, **runaways, throwaways, and other homeless children on their own are also without resources.** In 1986, approximately 75,000 youths were temporarily sheltered in 274 runaway facilities nationwide. However, estimates indicate that as many as 200,000 youths are homeless each year. Besides shelter, these youngsters need continuous support services. As many as 85 percent of America's homeless youth have suffered physical or sexual abuse (HHS Runaway and Homeless Youth Data). Annually, 60,000 children sixteen and older leave foster care. Shelters and runaway programs are designed for crisis intervention and family reunification. Such facilities cannot provide longer term care or comprehensive services to prepare homeless youth for independent living. Programs focused on independent living only became available in the last two years and meet as little as 15 percent of the need.

Ninth, **it is essential to prevent homelessness.** Recently, some funds have been used to prevent, rather than react to, homelessness. In New York, a new program called Housing Alert sends caseworkers to visit families to determine what additional services would strengthen their fragile living arrangements. "For some families, the key to preventing homelessness can be as simple as providing a sleep couch for a family doubled up with friends or relatives." (*The New York Times,* 6/9/87) NLC's 1986 Policy Working Paper, *Perspectives on Poverty,* points out potential local government and long-term preventive measures. In the short term, for example, laws protecting tenants against unnecesary evictions could be enacted or strengthened. In the long term, adequate and thorough documentation of the scale, composition, and trends concerning homelessness is essential. In addition, the creation of low-income housing can be leveraged through public/private partnerships, through wise use of properties gained through tax foreclosure, and through collaboration with employment programs to improve and renovate housing stock. Future designs must keep families and children in homes and provide them with services and resources to help them avoid becoming homeless.

The issues related to child and family homelessness are complex. There are no easy answers. The complexity requires comprehensive planning and a strong working partnership among all levels of government, the private sector, the service community, and the community at large.

Profiles

Policies and services to redress the problem must reflect the complexity of issues. The following profiles present different approaches to the problem. Included are programs that provide emergency shelter, transitional housing, "safe places", independent living, and short-term as well as long-term services. These programs serve a variety of populations — battered women and their children, low-income families, homeless youths who are runaways or throwaways, female-headed households, and children in public care without homes. The varied nature, geography and service populations of the programs illustrate the universality and diversity of issues related to child and family homelessness.

This is not to suggest these programs provide easy answers to the problem. Each community is unique and requires unique solutions to best address its problems. These profiles, however, illuminate some of the lessons learned in other communities. Space does not permit presentation of all the program options or population needs. Rather, the sample of programs in different communities demonstrates how some programs have sought to better meet the needs of homeless families and children. The aim is to share ideas and information that will give more communities the tools to meet the needs of their homeless children and families.

Washington, D.C.'s ConServe is a consortium of ten collaborating agencies that together offer a continuum of housing and support services that emphasize expanded access to the traditional housing market. Major funding is through a city contract for services the city itself can provide only at a much greater cost.

In West Chester, Pennsylvania, the Friends Association operates an emergency shelter for homeless families and offers a program aimed at preventing homelessness.

Chicago's Salvation Army-sponsored Emergency Lodge offers preschool education and child care services for children of homeless families using the emergency shelter and then follows up with a series of home visits after families find new homes in order to prevent future homelessness.

In Louisville, Kentucky, Project Safe Place is a unique outreach program that aims to prevent or alleviate homelessness among youth who are runaways or at risk in the streets.

Nashville, Tennessee is the home base for Oasis Center which includes one of the nation's few programs that prepares homeless teens for independent living.

Program Location	Population, Geography	Year Initiated	Budget	Municipal Involvement	Client Population	Services	Outcome Data	Comments
ConServe Inc. Washington, D.C.	638,432 east	1987	$325,000	Major funding through contract	50 homeless families per year	Transitional, permanent housing, case management	Monthly cost per family: $600; 1st year: 30 families in permanent housing	New approach consortium of agencies to provide coordinated and comprehensive services, including permanent housing
Friends Shelter-Townhouse West Chester, PA	20,000+ city and rural/suburban county, east	1982	$127,546	Service linkages	Homeless families and those at risk of homelessness	Emergency shelter, service referral and linkage	Housed 170 families each year since 1982. Bridge Housing + In-Home services = 275 homeless families helped	Linkage to Bridge Housing and in-home services beyond shelter placement
Salvation Army Nursery and Home Visiting Program Chicago, IL	3,005,070 midwestern	1982, Nursery; 1985, Home Visiting	$3,117 per child	Service linkages	children and families	Preschool education; home visits to prevent future homelessness	314 children in Nursery fiscal year 1987. 46 children and families in Home Visiting Program	The child and prevention are primary targets
Project Safe Place Louisville, KY	298,694 midwest	1983	$82,000	"safe" place locations, public relations, volunteers, some city $	Runaways, homeless youth: 150 per year	Community outreach, "safe places," crisis intervention, support services	240 "safe place" sites, 300+ homeless youth helped with short- and long-term services	Developed and implemented national model for "safe place" community outreach for homeless youth; national presidential award
Oasis Center Independent Living Program Nashville, TN	455,651 city and 12 counties south	1985	$250,000	Service links, positive public relations, community acceptance	Runaways, throwaways, youths in public care; 150/year; 10-12 living services in ILP at a time	Transitional and permanent housing and independent living services	15 teens in stable, permanent living situations; 12 teens moving to ILP	One of few programs providing independent living services and housing for homeless youth
Aurora House Toledo, OH	354,635 City and suburban county, central	1986	$70,000	Funding, technical assistance	Homeless women and families	Transitional housing and support services	First year: 25 women, 25 children in permanent housing; resource center services to 150+ women	Transitional facility with comprehensive employment services; cost effective
Winton House Wausau, WI	32,426; city and rural county, central	1986	$50,000/year/Rehab and $100,000 for operating $, house renovation	house and technical assistance	Battered women and their children	Transitional housing and support services	First year: 7 women., 12 children in permanent housing	Transitional facility for homeless women and families in non-metro area

Programs Dealing with Child and Family Homelessness

Aurora House in Toledo, Ohio, provides transitional housing for homeless women and their children for periods up to one year. A mix of private and public grants enables this non-profit agency to establish concrete plans for the long-term futures of its residents.

In Wausau, Wisconsin, Winton House is an example of a public/private partnership providing transitional living for women and children who are homeless because of domestic violence.

Concluding Remarks

What may be concluded from this overview of programs and problems related to child and family homelessness? First, child and family homelessness is a problem of crisis dimensions that will not simply go away. In fact, the evidence strongly suggests that child and family homelessness will continue to increase unless successful prevention and intervention programs are mounted.

Second, the best response to the problems of child and family homelessness is through comprehensive planning, design, coordination, and consolidation of resources, collaboration within and between communities, and solid working partnerships between the public and private sectors. The experience of some communities shows that these multiple ingredients can combine to break the cycle of homelessness. In February 1986, the City of Portland, Oregon, implemented a "12 Point Plan for the Homeless." (This effort has been profiled previously by NLC as part of the Second Annual City Innovation Conference in May 1987; *Proceedings* are available from NLC.) The effort was led by the mayor, the city council, and the county board of commissioners. The purpose was to mobilize the public and private resources of the City and County behind a wide-ranging plan to address homelessness. In May 1987, Portland's mayor reported the results: "One year later, here's the bottom line: The cycle of homelessness can be broken...There are no shortcuts, and breaking the cycle demands extensive time and funding..."

Third, adequate funding is a critical element in any design for more effective services. The cost of helping homeless families and children is high. But the future costs that result from not helping these families and children will be exorbitant.

Where will these funds come from? Some of the funds must come from government. Child and family homelessness is not an urban problem or a problem isolated in a few states. Child and family homelessness affects communities nationwide. Therefore, public funds must reflect a commitment shared across all levels of government. Cities, towns, rural boroughs, suburbs, counties, states, and the federal government must all participate in providing the necessary funds.

Private resources must likewise be mobilized. Some of the more effective approaches to child and family homelessness reflect creative consolidation of public and private funds. In Philadelphia, Denver, St.Paul, and other cities, the foundation community has provided the critical leadership in the design and funding of comprehensive programs for homeless families and children. In some communities, corporate support has been a major factor. Programs such as Louisville's Project Safe Place would find it difficult to survive without the financial support of the business community.

Fourth, increased citizen activism and political consciousness raising is needed. A candidate for local office in Maryland, made this need clear: "Broad-based citizen support will be needed to push politicians to take action. Most county residents do not feel that the [homelessness] problem is relevant to them...The only way we can begin to solve the problem is if we get support that something needs to be done." In spite of the statistics, many Americans remain unaware or unconvinced of the tragedy of child and family homelessness. This points out the continuing need to educate American society and government to the realities of child and family homelessness. So does a remark by San Francisco's Mayor Diane Feinstein, quoted in the *Washington Post* on November 1, 1987: "I think across the nation people have to come to grips with this: how can a country like ours be very proud when you have people sleeping next to ash cans?"

This chapter represents a small effort to provide some of the education so critical to defining better answers to the problem of child and family homelessness. Education will continue to be a key element in efforts to help America's homeless families and children. But all of the other ingredients are also essential— more funds, more community acceptance, more political responsibility, more citizen advocacy, more public/private partnership, and better design of policies and programs.

A list of references and resources follows the profiles on page 154.

ConServe: The Consortium for Services to Homeless Families
Washington, D.C.

Comprehensive services emphasizing permanent housing.

Contact:
Tony Russo, Executive Director,
ConServe Consortium,
1711 14th Street, N.W.,
Washington, D.C. 20009
202/ 232-3355

Ten collaborating service organizations working together as ConServe, Inc. are taking a dynamic new approach to addressing the complex problems of homeless families and children. The network of organizations offers homeless families a continuum of critical housing and support services with an emphasis on expanding the availability of low-cost rental units in the private sector.

Located in the District of Columbia, the consortium links the following provider organizations: Children's Hospital; Greentree Shelter; Community Family Life Services; For Love of Children; Hope and a Home; Housing Counseling Services; Jubilee Housing; Lutheran Social Services; Manna, Inc.; and, Samaritan Ministry. ConServe is the linchpin of the network, developing resources and service linkages, defining social contracts with the homeless families, providing case management and monitoring arrangements between families and provider.

ConServe is unique in a number of ways. The consortium model encourages the design of comprehensive services. Coordination and case management make it possible to carefully monitor family progress and the relevance of the consortium's services. The focus on permanent housing gives homeless families real opportunities to stabilize as families. The concept of a reciprocal social contract establishes solid criteria for evaluation of both family responsibilities and the accountability of the service network.

ConServe was established in February 1987. The consortium model seeks to reduce the costs of serving the homeless by eliminating expensive hotel stays and by providing comprehensive and coordinated services. The goals are to provide

123

adequate long-term housing and support services to keep homeless families intact and to build toward stable and productive futures.

Program referrals are accepted from the local shelters and the D.C. Department of Human Services (DHS). ConServe acts as case manager for each family, helping the family to define needs and matching services to the needs. The diagram below illustrates the straightforward sequence of intake and service arrangements:

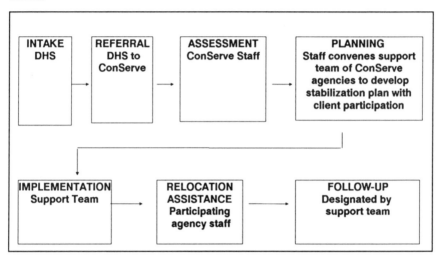

INTAKE DHS	REFERRAL DHS to ConServe	ASSESSMENT ConServe Staff	PLANNING Staff convenes support team of ConServe agencies to develop stabilization plan with client participation

IMPLEMENTATION Support Team	RELOCATION ASSISTANCE Participating agency staff	FOLLOW-UP Designated by support team

Housing is a critical core service for ConServe families. The program helps families locate permanent housing through consortium members and through development of private rental resources with District property owners. Because most homeless families cannot afford market rates for housing in the District of Columbia, ConServe has designed a private subsidy similar to the public Section 8 program. Homeless families contribute 30 percent of their gross income to the monthly rent. ConServe subsidizes and guarantees the rent difference, up to $300 per month.

The rent subsidy is contingent upon the family's adherence to a social contract. The contract, called the Family Stabilization Plan, establishes goals and responsibilities for families as well as for service providers. The plan includes elements such as employment, money management, education and training, child care and alcohol and drug counseling. Goals and time frames are mutually agreed upon. The ConServe case manager follows the family's progress and intervenes to provide needed services. Families who fail to work toward contracted goals will lose both the rent subsidy and consortium services. As described by a ConServe participant, "You have to set goals and show you're willing to stick to your goals." As of August 1987, no families had been terminated from the program.

ConServe's innovative approach has emerged at a crucial time. The District of Columbia government has been overwhelmed by the volume and extent of need of homeless families in the District. Vernon Hawkins, Deputy Commissioner of the District's Department of Human Services, has noted that requests for emergency shelter for homeless families increased by 500 percent in 1987. The number of homeless families is expected to increase by 20 percent in 1988. In 1987, DHS was confronted with requests for shelter that increased from thirty-five to fifty-six families a week. With its resources overwhelmed, the city's response has been an assortment of emergency shelters and "welfare" motels accompanied by fragmented services.

ConServe's entry into the D.C. service community has quickly established an alternative model for efficient and effective intervention to help homeless families and children. Since its inception in February 1987, ConServe has placed thirty homeless families in permanent private sector housing. Besides housing, the project has provided services that help families break the cycle of instability. More than half (53 precent) of the parents were helped to find employment or job training opportunities. Counseling and educational services have been provided to children who were not attending school or who were having academic problems. For some of the children, the improvements have been dramatic. The target for 1987 is to achieve successful housing placement and support services for more than fifty homeless families.

ConServe's service seems to indicate the cost effectiveness of the consortium approach. The city's monthly cost for minimum shelter and services to a homeless family is $2,700. ConServe's monthly cost for permanent housing and a spectrum of services for homeless families is $600 per month.

ConServe's dramatic success has been acclaimed by the media, the service and advocacy community, and the public at large. The project has produced tentative but compelling evidence that there is a cost-effective way to help break the cycle of homelessness for District families. The consortium approach is being followed by the staff of the Child Welfare League of America as a potential national model for improving services to homeless families. Dana Harris, Director of the Homelessness Information Exchange observes that "many programs offer emergency assistance .... ConServe's efforts lead to long-term stabilization for homeless families."

ConServe's first year operating budget is approximately $325,000. Nearly one-third of the budget, $105,000, is used for rental subsidies. Staffing and administrative costs make up the remainder of operating costs. At present, ConServe functions with only five staff positions: executive director, two case managers, a housing counselor, and a secretary.

The major source of revenue for the first year of operation has been a contract with the D.C. Department of Human Services. If the service contract continues, city funds may represent as much as 90 percent of ConServe's operating revenue. Other sources of support have been private foundation grants and individual contributions. The prognosis for second year funding is positive. Both the public and private sectors appear to be duly impressed by the program's early successes.

The most challenging aspect of ConServe's efforts to design effective intervention to help homeless families is to obtain adequate and affordable housing. In response, ConServe has developed a partnership with more than fifteen private property management companies in the metropolitan District of Columbia. The companies provide access to adequate, market-rate rental units. ConServe acts as the agent and intermediary between homeless families and the management companies. The innovative arrangement has proven effective in both client accountability and in building positive relationships with the private rental community. One property owner said, "It's the first program I've seen that works. We're getting people we like." (*Washington Times*, 5/4/87).

A central feature of ConServe's early efforts has been the consolidation and collaboration of critical resources, with permanent housing as the cementing element. The replicability of the consortium model is contingent upon the existence of community agencies with the capacity to serve homeless families. All of the ConServe agencies provided services to the homeless prior to becoming consortium members, but a lack of coordination among their differing services meant that homeless clients missed out on a lot of potential help. A second critical element is a community's ability to significantly expand low-income rental resources in the private sector. Without assertive housing advocacy and private sector linkages, even excellent consortium services will fail to remove families from homelessness.

Friends Shelter-Townhouse
West Chester, Pennsylvania

Emergency shelter and prevention services.

Contact:
Elaine K. Coate, Executive Director,
Friends Association for Care and Protection of Children (FACPC),
222 N. Walnut Street,
West Chester, PA 19380
215/ 431-3598-9

The Friends Association for the Care and Protection of Children (FACPC) can claim unusual historical relevance: 165 years after its origin, the organization continues to provide shelter and services to homeless children and their families. The Association was established in 1822 for the purpose of creating a network of homes for abandoned black children in Philadelphia. FACPC has developed new programs to meet changing needs, including services to families in their own homes to prevent homelessness, but the fundamental need to provide shelter for children has remained.

In 1982, FACPC opened an emergency shelter to house West Chester's homeless children and their families. The shelter is consistent with the 1822 intent of the Association "to provide not only shelter, food, and clothing but also loving attention and reasoned discipline to assist children...to realize their potentials as human beings and become productive members of society."

The shelter facility, known as the Friends Shelter-Townhouse, is located in downtown West Chester on the third floor of the YMCA building. The shelter has five bedrooms and may be stretched to accommodate up to three families of fourteen to fifteen people. The space is leased from the YMCA at an annual rental cost of approximately $15,000. The facility is well located to link homeless families with other community services.

The facility does not accept walk-in families. Homeless families are sent to community agencies for referral to the shelter. The screening process is a critical ingredient in cementing an immediate network of community services that may be needed by the families. The philosophy of the program is to address family homelessness in a holistic manner. Homeless families are seen as needing multiple, coordinated services. The program helps families to put the parts together to get what they need to establish their own homes.

West Chester is a borough of more than 20,000 people, about a half hour's drive from Philadelphia. The borough is located in Chester County, a rural Pennsylvania county with a population of 350,000 and an area of 761 square miles. The county is composed of the borough of West Chester, suburbs, small towns, and large rural areas. Historically, the county has been prosperous, but has pockets of persistent unemployment and poverty. In the 1980s, increasing numbers of county families have become homeless.

Who are West Chester's homeless families? According to Elaine Coate, FACPC's executive director, they are "abandoned or abused women", "families that are very much intact, but the man may have lost his job and they then lose everything", "families where there is alcohol, drugs, or illness" or "people who have looked high and wide for family housing for under $500 a month and can't find it." They are, she says, "families who are overwhelmed and defeated...and can't see a way out of their plight."

The emergency shelter offers homeless families and children an initial way out of their plight. Families may be sheltered for up to two weeks. Services are basic: food, shelter, crisis intervention and community linkage. During the limited stay, shelter staff and residents work quickly together to locate resources to meet the families' longer-term needs. Very often, however, the shelter's short stay disallows adequate time to truly resolve the homelessness. Since 1982, FACPC has added two programs to offer longer-term support, the Bridge Housing Program and the In-Home Services Program.

The Bridge Housing Program helps homeless families locate permanent, affordable, private sector housing. The program has established alliances with realtors and landlords to create a pool of more than twenty-five centrally located apartments with rents from $350 to $500. Help is also available for the pragmatic "nuts and bolts" of family resettlement, such as money for security deposits or overdue utility bills, furniture, cooking supplies and emergency food. The program provides a "bridge" of services and close supervision until families can stabilize income, budgeting, and family management. The program is able to serve up to twenty-five homeless families annually for periods from three months to one year.

The prevention-oriented In-Home Services Program takes a different, but complementary, approach. The program attempts to prevent homelessness by providing pragmatic counseling and support services to families in their own homes. Most clients receive weekly in-home counseling for at least three months and up to six months. Services address budgeting, household management, family relationships and definition of realistic educational and vocational goals to help parents achieve economic self-sufficiency. Children receive individualized services, directly through FACPC or through linkage with public service agencies. According to Ellen Coate, "The children are very important. They sometimes are the only resource that keeps a family together and motivated to move ahead."

Have the Friends Association programs helped West Chester families and children establish homes? It looks as if they have. Since opening in 1982, the Shelter-Townhouse has housed an average of 170 homeless women and children annually. In its first five years, only three families have requested re-entry to the shelter program. In 1987, the combined services of the shelter, the Bridge Program, and the In-Home Services Program helped more than 275 individuals to deal with family homelessness. FACPC's three core programs have worked in close concert with other community services. The functioning of the collaborative network of FACPC programs and community resources may itself be considered tangible evidence of the success of West Chester's efforts to help its homeless families.

Local government has consistently supported FACPC's efforts to help homeless families with funds and by participating in the service network. The Bridge Program is funded by state and county funds and coordinated by the Chester County Office of Human Services. FACPC also has purchase-of-service contracts with two other county agencies, the Housing Authority and the Drug and Alcohol Commission. Borough Mayor Tom Chambers is "glad they're available to us. We've learned from personal experience that they do high quality work."

A broad network of community resources has been mobilized on behalf of the homeless families. The network includes agencies such as the Health and Welfare Council of Chester County, the YMCA, the Women's Resource Center, the Salvation Army and Family Services of Chester County. The welding of government and private resources has been a key factor in the success of FACPC's efforts to resolve homelessness among West Chester families and children. In 1986, the Pennsylvania House of Representatives presented the association with a citation for its exemplary work on behalf of disadvantaged families and children.

The family shelter was a natural extension of FACPC's inventory of services for families and children. Still, homeless families represented new challenges. Locating adequate space was a first major step. As with any new service, start-up funds were a challenge. The first year support reflected the positive sharing between public and private resources. Seed funds were contributed by two Pennsylvania foundations and Chester County government, through a federal Title XX adult services block grant. With a location and funding, FACPC was able to move quickly to program design and staff recruitment.

The 1987-88 operating budget for the emergency shelter program is $127,546. The budget supports five staff positions: director; Town House administrator; Town House aide; Town House assistant; and secretary. All staff members participate in continuing skills training and educational development activities. Funding sources reflect a balance between public and private resources. Federal and county funds constitute 70 percent of revenue. The United Way, private foundations, and individuals contribute the remaining 30 percent.

A major barrier to FACPC's efforts to help West Chester's homeless families is the continuing inadequacy of resources. Homeless families, especially those headed by young single females, often lack both the social supports and the income to maintain stable living. As many as 50 percent of the homeless parents were homeless as children because their families were unstable or because they were in foster homes. The parents need training, education, and support services in order to achieve family stability and economic self-sufficiency.

Another major barrier is the lack of access to affordable housing. With limited incomes and poor references, young families cannot compete in the Chester County housing market. Also, local agencies serving the disadvantaged have often worked in isolation on pieces of problems of multi-problem families. As Ellen Coate says, "The important thing is networking and the ability to help financially and materially to settle people in permanent housing."

The FACPC programs and its concerted efforts to forge a public/private partnership represent a solid model for more effective services for homeless families and children. In the words of the director of the Chester County Office of Human Services, "The Friends Association program is an excellent example of the cooperation necessary between public and private resources to alleviate pressing community problems."

The Salvation Army
Nursery and Home Visiting Program
Chicago, Illinois

Services to help children and to prevent future family homelessness.

Contact:
Miriam Toelle, Director
800 W. Lawrence Avenue
Chicago, IL 60640
312/ 271-5773

The Salvation Army Nursery and Home Visiting Program provides unique services to homeless children and their families while they stay at The Salvation Army Emergency Lodge and after they move to new homes in order to prevent future homelessness.

The Emergency Lodge houses families that need temporary shelter because of crises in their lives. Although there is usually one single crisis—fire, eviction, domestic violence, or family disruption, among others—that causes the immediate need for shelter, many of the families have histories of transiency and instability. They are multi-problem families whose children are at risk.

Because the early years of life are so crucial to later growth and development, the Salvation Army Child Care Program began its own standard-model Head Start program at the Emergency Lodge. The Head Start program, started in 1979, served the three-to-five-year-old children of the homeless families at the shelter as well as children from the surrounding Uptown community. It was soon apparent that the children of homeless families were not best served by such a program because of the short-term nature of their stay at the Lodge and their particular needs and characteristics.

In the summer of 1982, the Child Care program received a Salvation Army-United Way allocation to open a separate program for the preschool children of families in the Lodge. Initially, there was a children's classroom program in the morning and a parents' program in the afternoon that centered around parent education. It did not take the staff long to realize that parents could not put their energies into such a program; their efforts went into finding housing, transferring

131

their public aid cases, and taking care of other business. An afternoon preschool session replaced the parents' session.

In January 1984, an informal home visiting program began, giving teachers an opportunity to help children make the transition from the shelter to their new homes and helping teachers with their feelings of loss and their concerns about the child's new situation. In December, 1985, with the help of a two-year Innovative Head Start grant, a formal home visiting program began. Since that time, the program has grown into a family support program that helps parents and children with the transition from homelessness to stability. The program is continuing with Head Start funding through the Chicago Department of Human Services. The Department's Commissioner, Judith Walker, is very supportive. "The Salvation Army's Head Start project addresses both in theory and in practice the critical educational and social service needs of homeless families with young children. The issue in dealing with homeless families must include more than mere shelters. We cannot allow our children to be thrown away."

The Nursery Program is based on the premises that children whose families are in crisis need special care and individual attention and that children cannot function appropriately if they are not equipped with the emotional skills necessary to attend to the world around them and to engage in productive activity. These children are often delayed in more than one area of development, but it is their extreme emotional and social vulnerability that forms the basis for program design. The Nursery is a safe, protective, nurturing, and supportive environment in which children begin to regain a sense of security, understand the reality of their situation, and reduce their stress.

Specifically, the program:

- supports parents by offering child care services;

- provides for the educational, physical, and socio-emotional needs of young children through the use of a child development curriculum model;

- makes teachers available to parents for any questions and concerns that parents may have about their children during their stay at the Lodge;

- provides opportunities for some parent education, informally, as appropriate;

- identifies children who may have special needs and refers them to appropriate agencies; and

- offers parents who establish a residence within the city a home visiting program after leaving the Lodge.

Children from three years old to kindergarten age may enroll in the Nursery. There are two sessions daily — a morning session from 8:30 to 11:30 and an afternoon session from 1:00 to 3:30 — and a Tuesday evening session so that mothers may attend the Women's Support Group.

The curriculum is based on the characteristic needs of children of homeless families. While egocentric behavior is typical of preschool children, it is magnified many times in these children. Recently, a four-year-old boy spent his first two days in the classroom lying across a box of small trucks so that he would not have to share his find with the other children. Most of the children are tired much of the time, and many have diarrhea. They have difficulty focusing on an activity, and they wander from area to area not knowing how to initiate play or accept the invitation of others. They tend to use toys and materials inappropriately, reflecting their lack of experience with them and the chaos and confusion in their lives. At snack time, they often gorge themselves, not from hunger, but from an emotional need.

The children often seem amazed by the choices they are offered in the classroom and the care they receive from the teachers. When it is time for dismissal they often cling to the teachers. Once they become comfortable in the classroom, their "truer" selves may emerge--more aggressive, more demanding, more intrusive.

The children are inappropriately affectionate toward strange adults. Yet relationships between children and mothers often seem to lack intimacy. Parents seem to possess limited parenting skills. Mothers and children separate easily; there is often no visible sign of physical contact or affection between them. Many times, these preschoolers are given the burden of caring for younger children.

Much time is spent on free play because this is such an important avenue for children in organizing and adjusting to their experiences. The use of dramatic play themes , including kitchen play, moving, and dress up, are encouraged, and appropriate materials are available.

The teachers must quickly and intensively establish a relationship with each child, knowing that it will be a short one and likely without closure. During each classroom session, the teachers engage each child individually as much as possible, encouraging them to speak about their feelings. They guide them to success in their activities while recognizing that children also need to feel competent. The teachers also help the children interact with other children.

A more difficult, but important task for teachers, is establishing a relationship of trust with the parents.

Recruiting for the Home Visiting Program begins when parents enroll their children in the shelter's child care program. Shortly after the children have enrolled in the classroom program, the teachers informally tell parents about the Home Visiting program and invite them to the weekly preschool parent meeting. The meeting gives parents an opportunity to talk about their children, to raise concerns about parenting, and to ask questions about the children's development, and it begins the creation of a trusting relationship between the Home Visiting Program staff and parents. Parents who attend the parent meeting generally enroll in the Home Visiting Program.

The Home Visiting Program is intended to reduce the incidence of transiency for the family and support the parent-child relationship. These goals, although simply stated, affect almost every aspect of the families' lives and must be set individually for each family.

The weekly home visits are made by a team, usually made up of a teacher and a social worker, who assess the education and social service needs of the children and parents and provide direct services and also link the family with community resources. The program for each child and family is based on individual goals designed to meet their specific needs.

Because of the many needs of parents and children and the constraints imposed by time and resources, the program focuses on some particular issues. For children, the emphasis is on enhancing their level of functioning by providing developmental activities, referral to Head Start, and evaluation and placement of children with special needs. For parents, the emphasis is on enhancing the parent-child relationship and helping the parent find and connect with community resources that will improve family stability.

Families with three- to-five-year-old children who took part in the preschool program while their family was at the shelter may apply to the Home Visiting program if they wish. Nursery attendance and family income are considered by the program staff in deciding on the applications; children with handicaps (as defined by Head Start), children that are abused or neglected, and children with mothers under the age of twenty-one are given special consideration.

Once the family leaves the shelter — where the average stay is only twenty-one days — and the visiting team is chosen, the home visits begin. They usually follow a pattern of three-month cycles, each made up of assessment, goal setting, implementation, and evaluation.

Assessment of both child and family takes place during the first four or five visits, using evaluations designed by the program staff and a standardized screening instrument for children.

Goal setting is done by the team. Each member of the team presents an assessment of the child and outlines steps that would benefit the child, and a family service plan is developed and agreed on.

Implementation of the plan takes place for about three months, during which the team members discuss the progress and problems of the children and parents and adjust the family goals, if necessary.

Evaluation begins with an assessment of the accomplishments during the three-month implementation period. Depending on the family's progress, the team may continue with the original goals or revise them.

The cycle of assessment, goal setting, implementation, and evaluation may be repeated three or four times—or more, if the family is making significant progress. If after six months, however, no family effort toward the family's goals is seen, the team may decide to break off the visits.

Once a month there is a Family Fun Night, a late afternoon/early evening (dinner is always served) event for parents and children. The activities can range from bingo (with donated prizes) to story telling to workshops on nutrition. Some activities are for parents, some for children, and some for the entire family.

The budget for the home visiting program includes a modest amount of money for helping families meet financial obligations or purchase needed items. Tokens for transportation are the most frequently purchased item.

Through its combination of children's and family services, preschool education, child care, and home visits, The Salvation Army Nursery and Home Visiting Program support children and families through the crises and transitions that come with homelessness.

The Nursery and Home Visiting Program is part of the Salvation Army's overall child care program, which encompasses various sites and programs. For further information, contact Alice Rose, Project Director, 1515 W. Monroe Street, Chicago, IL 60607; 312/733-2533.

A similar effort is the ALCOVE, a project operated by Child Care Dallas. The project is financially supported by the Jewish Coalition for the Homeless. It is designed to provide transitional child care for babies, toddlers, and preschoolers during the up-to-thirty days their parents may stay at the Downtown Family Shelter. The programmatic focus is on separation, affective education, and cognitive tracking and organization. For further information, contact Sonya Bemporad, Executive Program Director, Child Care Dallas, 1499 Regal Row, Suite 400, Dallas, TX 75247; 214/630-7911.

A second similar effort is the District of Columbia program that transports preschoolers from a shelter for the homeless to a Head Start program. For further information, contact Barbara Kamara, D.C. Office of Early Childhood Development, Randall Building, First and I Streets SW, Washington, DC 20024; 202/727-5930.

Miriam Toelle and Sheila Kerwin were the primary authors for the program description from which this profile has been adapted.

Project "Safe Place"
Louisville, Kentucky

Outreach and crisis intervention services.

Contact:
Elizabeth Triplett, Executive Director,
YMCA Center for Youth Alternatives
1410 S. First Street,
Louisville, KY 40208
502/ 635-5233

The YMCA Center for Youth Alternatives in Louisville, Kentucky offers a comprehensive program of shelter and services, including a 24-hour hotline, for children without homes. In 1983, the shelter launched a unique program, known as Project Safe Place, to provide outreach and crisis intervention services to prevent or alleviate homelessness among youth who are homeless, runaways, or at risk in the streets. In 1986, Safe Place was selected as one of thirty projects to receive the Presidential Award for Private Sector Initiatives.

The project is public/private partnership providing "safe places" and a range of services for homeless youth. Safe Place is exemplary because of the network of community "safe places" and the extensive involvement of corporate and individual volunteers. "Safe places" are settings in the Louisville community to which youngsters can go for temporary refuge and, if appropriate, transportation to a shelter for more extensive services. Safe places include a variety of community locations, such as fast food restaurants, public buildings, hospitals, fire stations, businesses and convenience stores. The locations are clearly identified by a large yellow "safe place" logo showing an adult embracing a child.

The program uses more than 150 volunteers as the first link to youngsters in need. Employees at the community locations serving as safe place sites are trained to identify, and communicate with, children who appear to need help. The employee ascertains the immediate situation and contacts the Center. A volunteer experienced in crisis intervention is immediately sent to the safe place site to help the youngster determine what to do next.

Project Safe Place is made possible through the extensive involvement of volunteers. Volunteers are carefully screened, including a police check and submission of character references. Those accepted must live within fifteen minutes of a safe place site and make a three-month commitment to on-call status. They also must participate in an orientation, an eight-hour certification class, and continuing skills training. Successful applicants tend to be mature, stable, quick-thinking, and non-judgmental. The Louisville project has been particularly successful in attracting senior volunteers, although the general age of volunteers ranges from twenty-eight to forty-five.

The concept of "safe places" was developed in 1983 by the Center's former executive director, Larry Wooldridge. Limited staff, lack of an outreach component, and lack of a means of transportation often prevented the shelter from responding to calls for help from youth in the community. Increasing numbers of runaways, homeless youth, and youths in crisis were not being helped because the shelter was unable to quickly link them with the help they needed. Project Safe Place was conceived as a way to provide speedy response, community involvement and expanded manpower in helping Louisville youth.

Who are "Safe Place" youngsters? They are runaways, homeless youths, and troubled youths, all of whom are vulnerable to injury and exploitation in the streets. A shelter counselor described them as "adolescents in the streets because of abuse, stepfamily issues, and/or emotional rejection and abandonment." They are youngsters without homes because of problems with family relationships or family economic problems. Wooldridge points out that "These aren't bad kids. They and their families are just struggling to cope."

Since its beginning, Project Safe Place has expanded to more than 240 sites in the Louisville area. The easy access to safe places has made it possible to help youths in the early stages of crisis, and the early intervention has prevented or quickly ameliorated homelessness. Half of the safe place youths have remained at the shelter for one day or less, and another 20 percent needed shelter services for periods of only two days to a week. Most returned home; those without homes or with unworkable family situations have gone to foster families or the ILP group dorm. By 1987, the program has helped more than 300 homeless and at-risk youngsters find short-term shelter and obtain longer-term services to assure future stability.

The city government has played a major role in the evolution and expansion of Project Safe Place. From the beginning of the project, a significant number of safe place settings were public facilities. The city government has actively promoted public awareness and helped mobilize community volunteers. City funds provided seed monies for the opening of the YMCA's Shelter House in 1974. Through the years, the city and the YMCA have maintained a positive working relationship to better meet the needs of Louisville youth.

Besides providing critical, concrete services for homeless and at-risk youth, the project has been a major catalyst for expanded community collaboration in addressing the needs of Louisville families and children. In its first two years, Project Safe Place has generated positive feedback and community support from a variety of sources:

> "The United Way sees Safe Place as one of its shining lights."

> From a convenience store sponsor, "Being part of the project is a way of giving something back. It gives the stores a chance to help out their neighbors and really be a part of the community.. ...It's a definite community need".

> From a corporate supporter, "I realize now there's a lot more to the YMCA than just going down once a week to swim."

> From the President of the United States, "The Awards Committee was very impressed by your organization's commitment to extending a helping hand to your community, selecting you from more than 1,500 projects nationwide."

The Louisville school system has "adopted" the project and actively pursues an awareness campaign within the educational community. By 1987, more than 40,000 young people had been informed about the project. The media have also developed an continuing campaign to publicize children's issues. The project has received national attention and is being replicated in other locations, including Oasis Center in Nashville, Tennessee; the city of Gary and eight Indiana counties; the Chicago, Illinois area; Madison, Wisconsin; and Montgomery, Alabama. The diverse locations support the contention that the project is replicable in a variety of communities.

Project Safe Place operates on an annual budget of $82,000. A staff of two assumes all responsibility for delivering services and coordinating of volunteers. From 150 to 200 volunteers participate annually. The project's funds come from all levels of government and a variety of private resources. Major seed funds were provided by a federal Runaway and Homeless Youth Act grant, which was matched with city funds. The state and county also provide support through their youth and social services departments. Local government funds will be gradually withdrawn in 1988, as the United Way, corporations, individual contributors, and other private sources become primary sources of revenue for the project.

A major barrier to developing shelter and services for homeless and at-risk youth has been the public's lack of awareness of the dimension and complexity of the problem. A significant outcome of Project Safe Place has been an increased community awareness and collaboration to address the needs of children without homes. The Project shows what can be achieved through effective public/private partnership.

Project Safe Place offers a unique model for expanding services to homeless children and their families. The project can be replicable in any community in which there is a residential shelter facility for youth. Although the Louisville project has more than 240 sites, smaller communities may do the same thing with many fewer safe places. The Louisville model began with a staff of one and an operating budget of $15,000. Partial replications may involve community sites with informational posters and free phone calls for youth seeking shelter. Fellowship of Lights, a youth shelter in Baltimore, Maryland, has experimented with partial replication (1300 North Calvert Street, Baltimore, Maryland 21201, Ross Pologe, Executive Director; (301) 837-8155).

Organizations interested in replicating Project Safe Place may obtain a comprehensive packet of materials from the National Resource Center for Youth Services, University of Oklahoma, 131 North Greenwood Avenue, Tulsa, Oklahoma 74120; 918/585-2986. The Louisville staff can also provide information on using senior volunteers involvement in safe place projects.

Oasis Center Independent Living Program
Nashville, Tennessee

Independent living services for homeless youths.

Contact:
Della Hughes, ACSW, Executive Director
Oasis Center, Inc.
1219 16th Avenue South
P.O. Box 121648
Nashville, TN 37212
615/ 327-4455

Since 1985, Oasis Center has offered an innovative program of shelter and services for homeless youths and teens who are "graduating" from the public child welfare system. Known as the Independent Living Program (ILP), it is one of only a few programs nationwide that provide independent living services for youths. Oasis Center is located in Nashville, Tennessee, but it serves a broad area including thirty diverse counties. The center houses the only 24-hour walk-in shelter in middle Tennessee for homeless and troubled teens.

A note from a 17-year-old Oasis Center youth tells why the program is important:

> "Dear President Reagan, I am in the Department of Human Services' custody and have been for a year now. I was a runaway for four years because no one cared for me and people kept on putting me in group homes and institutions...The world has helped homeless that are adults, so why not help young people that are homeless? All it takes is a home with loving people that care."

The Oasis Independent Living Program offers "all it takes" to alleviate homelessness among youths and to prepare them for stable and self-sufficient futures. The purpose of the program is to assist homeless youths and youths in public care to achieve the skills and strengths for independent living. Some of the youngsters enter the program through the emergency shelter, which offers thirty-day stays and a range of crisis intervention, family stabilization and outreach services.

The program provides four phases of services, geared to meet the differing needs of homeless youth: intensive services to deal with abuse, hostility, poor self-esteem, and/or poor school performance; information, skill development, and placement with a support family that permits some independence within a structured environment; shared apartment living, to provide transition into independent living with a minimum of supervision from a resident manager; and after-care to provide minimal counseling and assistance with networking after graduation from ILP. Two types of living arrangements are available — family support homes and a ten-bed supervised, group living facility.

The goal for youngsters without homes is graduation to living on their own in stable environments. Adolescents who become involved in the Independent Living Program, like many of the youths served by Oasis Center programs, are at high risk. They have many characteristics in common: they are often low-income youths, high school dropouts, illegitimate, vicitms of physical or sexual abuse (estimated at 95 percent of the youths in public care and two-thirds of those who are homeless), have few or no skills, and are substance abusers or from families with histories of substance abuse.

Youths in the Independent Living Program have typically lived in many public placements or in the streets, and they face multiple barriers to independent living. Della Hughes, the executive director, points out that "These are multi-problem youth who need intensive staff support, while providing a safe place for old wounds and experiences to heal." Regardless of the problem histories, the program's philosophy is that with good services these youth can learn to take control of their lives and become responsible adults.

The federal Runaway and Homeless Youth Act has been a major catalyst for expansion of state and local programs for runaway and homeless youths. The act provides funds for the National Runaway Switchboard and 286 youth shelters nationwide, including the Oasis Center emergency shelter. Most shelter programs, however, focus on short-term crisis intervention and family reunification. Their facilities are ill-equipped to offer transitional services that can help young people become capable of living independently. In 1983-1984, the first federal funds became available for states and localities to design youth independent living projects. The new federal monies helped to expand services within the Oasis Center's Independent Living Program.

Since its opening in 1985, the Oasis Center Independent Living Program has "graduated" fifteen teens. Before leaving, the youths were helped to locate housing, employment, social services, education and family support systems. The program has provided after-care and follow-up services for periods up to two years to assure continued stability. Ten support families have been recruited to offer interim and longer-term living arrangements for youths without homes. Twelve youths are in various stages of preparation for movement to independent living. Overall, in 1987, the combined efforts of the shelter and the Independent Living Program have prevented or ameliorated homelessness for more than 150 Tennessee youngsters.

The total operating budget for all Oasis Center programs exceeds $1.25 million and supports a staff of seventy. It reflects collaborative funding from both public and private sources. More than $350,000 in federal funds support independent living, emergency shelter, and employment components. Funds from the state departments of Human Services, Mental Health, and Juvenile Justice contribute more than $525,000. The United Way has contributed over $240,000, and individuals, corporations, and foundations have provide some $75,000. About 10 percent of the program's operating costs are covered by program service fees.

The 1987 budget for the Independent Living Program is approximately $250,000 and supports eight staff members. The original seed funds for the program were provided by a contract with the Tennessee Department of Human Services. Currently, federal funds support approximately 50 percent of ILP costs. State grants through departments of human services and juvenile justice contribute amounts equivalent to the federal share. ILP uses many of the services available in other Oasis Center youth programs.

The Independent Living Program has benefited from a close working relationship with community resources. Linkages with a broad spectrum of youth and family service agencies assure that ILP youths obtain needed services. In 1985, a major grant from the Robert Wood Johnson Foundation allowed expansion of health care services to ensure that homeless youth could be served.

The major barriers to delivering effective independent living services to homeless and troubled youths are often the characteristics of the youngsters themselves. Young people who have been in the streets or in public care for extensive periods may lack sufficient developmental and relationship skills to function well on their own. These youths resist caring about anything, distrust adults, and generally hide their feelings from the external world. They lack both the tangible skills (such as budgeting and locating jobs and housing) and intangible skills (such as building self-esteem and interpersonal relationshps, and decision making) needed for adult living. The Independent Living Program deals with this wide range of needs to give youngsters a fundamental base for stable and productive futures.

Two members of the Oasis Independent Living Program staff have contributed a chapter in a book designed to help other organizations design independent living programs. The guide, *Pathways to Adulthood: Creating Successful Programs to Prepare Troubled Teens for Independence*, summarizes the major barriers to building successful programs and ways they can be surmounted. It is available from the National Resource Center for Youth Services, University of Oklahoma, 131 North Greenwood Avenue, Tulsa, Oklahoma 74120; 918/585-2986.

Although they are few in number, there are other independent living programs that may also serve as models. In Boston, the Bridge House Transitional Living Project offers independent living services for homeless youths and pregnant teens (27 Litchfield Street, Brighton, MA 02135; 617/787-4364, Daniel Henderson, Program Director). The Illinois Self Sufficiency Program for Older Homeless Youth is a replication of the Ohio Advocate Home Network Model. The program serves homeless youth, runaways, and adolescents in public care (Department of Children and Family Services, 100 W. Randolph Street, Suite 6200, Chicago, IL 60601; 312/917-4152, Deborah Bridgeforth, Project Director). Perhaps the oldest model is found in Michigan, the Supervised Independent Living Program. Sponsored by the Michigan Department of Social Services and the Youth Living Center, Inc., the program provides transitional services to youths aged sixteen to eighteen who have resided in public care institutions (2 Town Square, Wayne, MI 48184; 313/729-8945, Barry Manning, Director).

Aurora House
Toledo, Ohio

Transitional housing for homeless women and children.

Contact:
Sister Dorothy Nussbaum, RSM, Executive Director
Aurora House
738 South St. Clair
Toledo, OH 43609
419/241-7975

Aurora House is a new program that offers transitional housing and independent living services for homeless women and their children. The program bridges a critical gap between short-term emergency shelter and permanent housing. Located in Toledo, Ohio, the home is the only facility in Lucas County that provides homeless families with transitional living for periods up to one year. Families who come homeless to Aurora House leave with homes and concrete plans for stable and self-sufficient futures.

Central to the program's philosophy is helping homeless women to help themselves break the cycle of poverty and dependency. The purpose is to help each resident define both short- and long-term goals to construct new futures for themselves and their children. "Aurora," the Latin word for dawn, symbolizes the focus on new beginnings for program residents. The new beginnings exist within the supportive home environment and in individualized services for each woman and her children. An on-site resource center offers a range of pragmatic services, including GED referral, career assessment, skills development, resume writing, job hunting and child care advocacy.

The facility was carefully designed and developed over a three-year period. In 1985, the Aurora Project became a non-profit corporation. The executive director, Sister Dorothy Nussbaum, was recruited from the Sisters of Mercy, an order whose lengthy history of helping disadvantaged women began with the establishment of a house for displaced women in Dublin, Ireland in 1827. In Toledo 159 years later, the need still exists, and within a week of its opening in September 1986, Aurora House was filled to capacity and had to turn away applicants.

In 1982, the city and community agencies organized a Women's Task Force to assess the needs of disadvantaged women in the Toledo area. A task force survey found that nearly one-third of female-headed households in Lucas County had incomes of less than $7,300, approximately one-third of the median income of county two-parent households and well below the national poverty index. Women indicated significant need for help related to housing, employment and education. The Toledo findings matched the national trend in the feminization of poverty. The dramatic statistics regarding unmet needs of Toledo female-headed households became a major impetus for development of Aurora House.

Aurora's women face formidable barriers to independent living. The majority of the first-year residents lacked both income and social supports to sustain stable living. More than 50 percent of the residents had no source of income and were referred, at least temporarily, to public assistance programs. The women also lacked adequate education and skills or experience to obtain meaningful employment. As portrayed by Jackie Parker, Aurora Board President, these are "multi-problem women, socially and economically disadvantaged women, who don't fit into nice categories".

According to Sister Nussbaum, the goal of Aurora House is "to help women ... get back in the mainstream". The house is located in a former convent building that is leased from SS. Peter and Paul Parish. The home can accommodate seven women and ten children up to the age of ten. Stays may vary from a few weeks to one year, as long as residents are actively working toward independence. The program hopes to serve approximately fifty women and their children during 1987-1988. Additionally, a resource center and outreach program anticipates helping 150 women through advocacy and support services related to housing, employment and career education.

Early indications are that Aurora House is effective in helping its disadvantaged women break the cycle of homelessness. Since its opening in September 1986, Aurora House has achieved new beginnings for twenty-nine women and twenty-five children. The new beginnings included permanent housing and resources for economic independence and emotional stability. As families returned to the community, Aurora House has continued to provide followup and outreach services through the resource center.

The success of Aurora's first year may be seen in continued city and community support as well as in the progress of its residents. The facility has been accepted by the local neighborhood, and community residents participate in some of the programs offered by the Aurora Resource Center. The Junior League of Toledo is considering Aurora House as a priority project for 1988. The city is providing technical assistance related to Aurora's possible purchase of the building it uses. Perhaps the most important indicator of Aurora's success, however, is that the development of an Aurora II transitional facility is being discussed seriously.

The first year's operating budget for the project exceeds $70,000. Staffing is lean. There are only five positions: a project director and a night manager, both full-time positions, and a program director, secretary, and bookkeeper, all part-time positions. Start-up costs were kept low by extensive volunteer help in rehabilitation and by significant contributions of furniture and other tangible items. More than thirty volunteers provide staff support and allow expanded resident services. Both staff and volunteers participate in program and resource center training related to working with the disadvantaged.

The funding base is diverse. The city's Office of Community Development contributed two grants, each of approximately $10,000. Hands Across America awarded $5,000 to the project. United Way Special Projects provided $15,000 in seed funds. The Sisters of Mercy gave $5,000 to start the program. Private foundations and individual contributors supported nearly 40 percent of the first year's funds. Finally, residents themselves contribute to program operation. As feasible, residents pay one-third of their income for rent and may apply their food stamps to residence costs.

The prognosis for future funding is good, although Aurora House recognizes that the program will always be challenged to obtain support. "Much of my time in the next few months will be spent applying for grants and seeking other funds for the project," the executive director says. More than 50 percent of Aurora's residents are unable to contribute at all, and 20 percent manage only partial payment. The city has been generous in the past, and it has a positive relationship with the program. At present, no federal funds other than resident food stamps have been tapped.

There are many challenges to developing effective transitional programs for homeless families. Solid planning and design takes time. Aurora House took nearly four years to become a reality. Locating an adequate structure in a supportive community may be difficult. For Aurora House, the city government's support and the leadership of the Women's Task Force were crucial. Other transitional projects nationwide report that community opposition may perhaps be the major barrier to implementation of programs. In some cases, neighborhood opposition has spanned a decade or prevented projects altogether.

A second major barrier to building transitional programs for homeless families is the lack of both seed funds and ongoing operating expenses. As with any new service, new programs face fierce competition for start-up funding. If they succeed in obtaining initial support, programs must then immediately concentrate on developing adequate future funding. Aurora faces that challenge in its second year. Setting a balanced and diversified fund base early in the program may help to provide a varied base of support in the future.

A third major barrier to effective transitional services for homeless families is the lack of affordable, permanent housing. Transitional programs offer only interim solutions to homelessness. Stays at facilities such as Aurora House may help homeless parents to increase their employability as well as to accumulate monies for security deposits and rent. When these families are ready to move out of transition, however, there must be a place for them to go. The Aurora project provides ample help in obtaining housing for its clients through linkage with public resources and through development of private sector contacts. Transitional facilities must address issues of access to affordable, permanent housing if homeless families are to make successful transition back into the community.

In its development and implementation, Aurora House has met challenges and overcome barriers. At least four sets of factors may be directly related to the project's beginning success: careful design and planning; strong leadership by the Women's Task Force; city and community support; and the patience, dedication, and hard work of the sponsoring organization.

Aurora House represents a solid model for transitional housing and support services that can give homeless families and children new starts. The project could be replicated in small or large communities and in urban, suburban, and rural areas. An excellent resource, *A Manual on Transitional Housing*, is available to organizations interested in the development of transitional facilities for homeless women and families. It may be obtained from The Women's Institute for Housing and Economic Development, Inc., 179 South Street, Boston, Massachusetts 02111; (617) 423-2296.

Winton House
Wausau, Wisconsin

Transitional living program for women and their children who are homeless because of domestic violence.

Contact:
Phyllis Bermingham, Executive Director
The Women's Community, Inc. (TWC)
329 Fourth Street
P. O. Box 1502
Wausau, WI 54401
715/ 842-5663

Winton House, located in Wausau, Wisconsin, is the only transitional facility serving the homeless in central Wisconsin. The program allows women and their children who are homeless because of domestic violence to stay in one of the building's five apartment units for up to a year. By definition, a transitional facility bridges the gap between the crisis creating the homelessness and a long-term solution. Such a facility goes beyond emergency shelter by providing both housing and support services over a period of time long enough to deal with all the problems in the way of a long-term solution.

Sponsored by The Women's Community, Inc. (TWC), the Transitional Living Program (TLP) demonstrates a public/private partnership that helps homeless families. The Women's Community, the City of Wausau, local private lenders, the Wisconsin Housing and Economic Development Authority, the Wausau Housing Authority, businesses, a local foundation, and numerous city residents joined together to make Winton House a reality. As explained by Connie Chilicki, Wausau Community Development Director, "Wausau, by geographic location, is a city that must do many things on its own; people pride themselves on that fact but also that we 'do it alone — together.' There is an effective partnership approach to meeting community needs."

The Transitional Living Program began in 1985 as an outgrowth of The Women's Community emergency shelter program for victims of domestic abuse. The shelter offered critical crisis services, but short-term intervention often failed to keep battered women and children from returning to the violent environment. According to Phyllis Bermingham, executive director of The Women's Community, "53 percent of the women returned to the abusive situation. We found that after we helped them [with the immediate shelter crisis], there was no support system available." Without a structured program after leaving the abusive relationship, the women lacked financial and emotional supports to build new futures. Transitional services became a critical link for defining longer-term resolution of family instability and homelessness.

The Women's Community is a private, non-profit organization established in 1978 to "meet the emerging needs of area women." TWC focuses on three program areas: sexual abuse/assault services; comprehensive domestic abuse services; and, employment training for disadvantaged women. The purpose of all services is to increase the economic self-sufficiency of women and to improve the quality of family life. The organization has grown from an all-volunteer drop-in center to a major human service agency with a staff of fifteen. TWC serves a mixed urban and rural population, drawn from three cities and Marathon County.

Winton House, a century-old building in Wausau, provides the housing for TWC's Transitional Living Program. The building was rehabilitated to provide five apartments: two self-contained two-bedroom units and three efficiencies with a communal kitchen and bath. The purpose of the project is to offer affordable, secure, attractive living units and support services to help battered women and their children to make the transition to emotional and economic self-sufficiency.

Residents may lease the units for up to a year at reduced rents. All tenants establish a written contract that outlines self-sufficiency goals and a specific plan for meeting them. Besides participation in transitional living services, other requirements for occupancy include no alcohol or drugs, no spousal abusers on the premises, no overnight guests without staff approval, and demonstrated progress toward self-sufficiency goals.

The TLP offers a spectrum of intensive services for the women and their children. Referrals are received from other TWC programs (such as crisis domestic abuse), from community services, and from self-referral. Special services for children are contracted from the Children's Service Society of Wisconsin. Women's services, in coordination with The Women's Community, include individual counseling, support groups, advocacy, community referral, and employment assistance through the TWC's New Options for Women program. The New Options program offers skills and training to help low-income women locate meaningful employment. Coordination with community resources is a key component of TLP, especially with departments of social services, family law attorneys, the criminal justice system, and local housing and employment sources.

Have TLP's services been effective? Program statistics, media reports, and city and community support suggest that they have. Since June 1986, Winton House has served seven women and twelve children. None of the residents has been asked to leave. Those that have left the project left because they no longer needed transitional living services. So far, not one woman has returned to an abusive relationship.

Who are the clients? This composite describes the typical Winton House resident:

> Rural Marathon County resident with two children. Entered crisis shelter. Toward end of maximum one month stay made decision to leave abusive marriage of six years. Became involved with Transitional Living Program for self and children. Entered Winton House. Completed TWC's employment program and enrolled in two-year technical training program at local community college. After nine months left Winton House for other rental housing. Continues to participate in Transitional Living Program services and credits these services for new belief in her ability to be self-sufficient.

Although the numbers are small, the results present sound evidence of the success of the Transitional Living Program. Other indications of the program's effectiveness come from the surrounding community and the local news media. The community has continued to be overwhelmingly supportive. In February 1987, a local television station did a three-part series about the project entitled "Picking Up the Pieces". The series and consistent positive media and newspaper coverage has attracted volunteers, materials, and funds. The prognosis for future funding appears to be very good, based on the solid working partnership of The Women's Community with city and state governments, local business and community groups, and the provider network.

The Winton House building cost $60,000. Funds for the purchase came from three sources: the Wisconsin Housing & Economic Development Authority contributed $25,000; the city's Community Development Department contributed $25,000; and The Women's Community arranged a $10,000 mortgage with a private lending institution. The rehabilitation cost approximately $40,000. The Wausau Community Development Department contributed the majority of rehabilitation funds, as well as critical staff support for technical assistance. The rehabilitation was done at reduced rates by local contractors, augmented by hundreds of hours of volunteer work. The majority of furniture, equipment, and supplies was donated by hundreds of individual and corporate contributors. More than a thousand volunteer hours have sustained the Transitional Living Program with both direct and support services.

The considerable volunteer and community investment in the building's rehabilitation has continued into program delivery and has kept the program's operating costs moderate. The annual budget includes $50,000 from a state health and social services grant. Rental income from residents pays the monthly mortgage payment. The program borrows many staff services from the professional staff of The Women's Community. The emergency shelter and employment services are supported by city funds, by state funds from the Wisconsin Department of Health and Social Services, by county funds from the Marathon County Private Industry Council, and by the local United Way. Four positions are directly connected to the transitional project: the executive director of The Women's Community, one-quarter time; program manager, full-time; assistant manager, half-time; and business manager, one-quarter time.

The Transitional Living Program can look back at a successful first year for the people it serves, its staff, and the community at large. The major barriers to successfully serving families who are homeless because of domestic violence echo issues raised by other programs. In Wausau, as in communities throughout the United States, there is a serious shortage of adequate and affordable housing. Women and children who have been homeless have neither the money nor the resources to locate stable housing. Families that have suffered from domestic violence and homelessness need much time and service investment in order to bounce back to emotional and economic stability. Without good comprehensive services, these families may face a costly sequence of episodes of homelessness. Short-term or isolated programs may be doomed in their efforts to help abused women and their families break the cycle of dependency. What seems necessary are compassionate, relevant, and pragmatic services that actually solve the problems of family instability, domestic violence, and homelessness. The Women's Community Transitional Living Program is concrete proof that such an approach works.

There are some similar transitional programs for families who are homeless because of domestic violence, but the need far exceeds the resources. Second Step Housing in San Rafael, California, offers a ten-unit residence and a range of counseling, training, and support services for battered women and their children. In Austin, Texas, the Center for Battered Women operates a unique program which provides abused women and their children with comprehensive services and transitional housing in scattered site apartments throughout the city. A Boston organization, the Women's Institute for Housing and Economic Development, Inc., offers an excellent guide which discusses these and other transitional projects in the U.S. and worldwide. *A Manual on Transitional Housing* offers comprehensive information about the design of effective transitional housing programs for homeless women and families and may be obtained by calling or writing: The Women's Institute for Housing and Economic Development, Inc., 179 South Street, Boston, Massachusetts 02111; 617/423-2296.

References

Bassuk, E. et al. 1986. "Characteristics of Sheltered Homeless Families", *American Journal of Public Health*, 76(9): 113-17.

Bassuk, E. 1986. "Homeless Families: Single Mothers and Their Children in Boston Shelters", *The Mental Health Needs of Homeless Persons*. San Francisco: Jossey-Bass.

Bucy, June. 1987. "Testimony before U.S. House of Representatives Select Committee on Children, Youth, and Families." February 24, 1987. Washington, D. C.: National Network of Runaway and Youth Services.

Children's Defense Fund. 1987. *A Children's Defense Budget*. Washington, D. C.

Democratic Study Group. 1987. "Special Report: The Homeless: Myths vs. Reality." Washington, D.C.

Goldberg, K. and Montague, W. "'Shelter Kids' — Homeless Children Posing Special Problems for Educators, Policymakers, Social Workers." *Education Week*, 6(30): 4/22/87.

Gorman, Paul. "Busy Being Born: Homes for the Homeless", *Cathedral*, News of the Cathedral of St. John the Divine, 2(2): March, 1987.

Henry, Neil. "A School with No Name", *The Washington Post*, 6/21/87.

Maza, P. and Hall, J. Undated. "Study of Homeless Children and Families: Preliminary Findings." Child Welfare League of America and Travelers Aid International.

McChesney, K. Y. 1986. "Families: The New Homeless", *Family Professional*, 1(1): 13-14.

National Coalition for the Homeless. "National Coalition Fact Sheet Info: Who, Why, How Many, and How Much?", *Safety Network*, May, 1987.

National Institute of Building Sciences. 1987. *Meeting America's Housing Needs*. Washington, D. C.

National League of Cities. 1987. *A Time to Build Up: A Survey of Cities about Housing Policy*. Washington, D.C

National League of Cituies. 1986 *Perspectives on Poverty: Issues and Options in Welfare Reform, Health Care and Homelessness*. Washington, D.C.

City of Portland, Oregon. 1987. *Breaking the Cycle of Homelessness: The Portland Model*. Portland, (OR): Office of the Mayor.

U.S. Conference of Mayors. 1987. *A Status Report on Homeless Families in America's Cities*. Washington, D. C.

U.S. Department of Health and Human Services. 1987. "An Occasional Report on Runaway and Homeless Youth Data, Summary Data on Homeless Youth." Washington, D. C.: Family and Youth Services Bureau, Program Operations Division.

U.S. Department of Housing and Urban Development. 1984. *A Report to the Secretary on the Homeless and Emergency Shelters*. Washington, D. C.: Office of Policy Development and Research.

U.S. General Accounting Office. 1985. *Homelessness: A Complex Problem and the Federal Response*. Washington, D.C.

U.S. House of Representatives. *The Crisis in Homelessness: Effects on Children and Families*. Hearing before the Select Committee on Children, Youth, and Families. 100th Congress, First Session, February 24, 1987. Washington, D. C.: U. S. Government Printing Office.

Women's Institute for Housing and Economic Development, Inc. 1986. *A Manual on Transitional Housing*. Boston.,

Wright, J. 1987. "Prepared statement" in report of hearing before U.S. House of Representatives Select Committee on Children, Youth, and Families. 100th Congress, First session, February 24, 1987. Washington, D. C.: U. S. Government Printing Office.

Organizations

Homeless Information Exchange
1120 G Street NW
Washington, D.C. 20005
202/628-2981
Dana H. Harris, Director

The Exchange provides information and technical assistance on programs for the homeless, including program summaries, bibliographies, and funding information. It identifies effective policy development and helps organizations conduct assessment and feasibility studies and build coalitions.

National Coalition for the Homeless
105 East 22nd Street
New York, NY 10010
212/460-8110

The Coalition is a federation of organizations and individuals around the country. It publishes a newsletter called *Safety Network*, which features legislative and programmatic information concerning the homelessness issue.

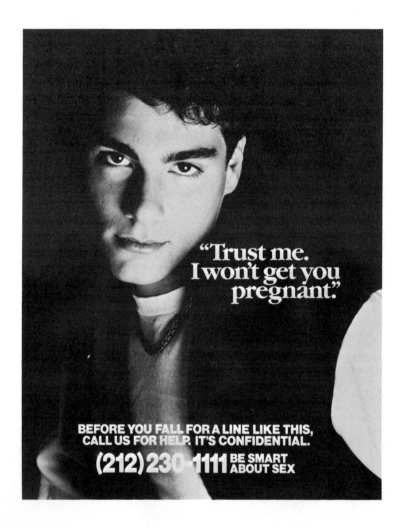

New York teens can trust the New York City Office on Adolescent Pregnancy and Parenting Services to give them help and advice. This poster is part of the city campaign to prevent teen sexual activity and teen pregnancy. For further information about the campaign, call 212/566-3450. Used with permission.

Chapter VI

Adolescent Pregnancy Prevention

Karen J. Pittman
Sharon Adams-Taylor
Mary Morich

> *"(I got) pregnant at 12. They say that's nothing now. When I was in the hospital there was a girl, 9. She had an 8-pound baby." Tiffany, age 14, mother of two*
>
> *"Babies Having Babies,"*
> *Miami Herald, February 10, 1986*

Tiffany and 10,000 other teens fourteen and younger have children each year in America. But they represent only one of the many faces of the teen pregnancy problem. For every Tiffany who gives birth, two pregnant girls fourteen or younger have abortions. To these teenagers must be added the teenage mothers on welfare, the teen fathers dropping out of schools, the young men who are out of school and unemployed, those who, while employed, cannot earn enough to support a family, and the staggering number of young families living in poverty. Together, they show that the problem of teen pregnancy transcends all facets of society.

Most of these pregnant and parenting teens are white. Poor and minority teens, however, have a disproportionate share of teen births: a black teen is twice as likely to become pregnant as a white teen, a fact primarily correlated to higher poverty rates among black teens.

These teens don't live only in big cities. In fact, 65 percent of the births to teenagers occur in cities with populations less than 100,000.

The teen pregnancy problem changes from community to community; it requires local analyses and local solutions. These tailored solutions, however, need a common understanding of why adolescent pregnancy is a problem and what cities can do about it.

Background

In 1985, there were 308,000 births to teens eighteen and under, including 10,000 to teens under fifteen. Each day 844 babies are born to young women eighteen and under who should be in school.

These numbers are certainly sobering, but do they alone point to a problem? No. There have always been teenage mothers and teenage fathers. In fact, if one looks at the numbers alone, the teen pregnancy problem seems to be diminishing. The number of babies born to teens in fact has been dropping steadily since the mid-1970s. Because of a decrease in the number of adolescents and a fall in the proportion of adolescents having babies, the number of births to teens fell below 500,000 in 1983 for the first time since before 1960. What has converted an old biological phenomenon into a new economic and social crisis is not an increase in the number or rate of teen births, but a change in what our society requires of teens as they make the transition from adolescence to adulthood — a change in the price they pay if they deviate from that path. Today, timing is everything.

Becoming a parent and leaving school are both important and expected marks of adulthood, but they are steps in a well-established sequence. We expect teens to finish their schooling, settle into a job, and marry before they begin raising a family. Clearly, however, teen parents do not take these steps in the expected order, and in fact, many do not even go through some of the expected stages:

- Half of the teen women who had children before the age of eighteen never complete high school.
- Half of the babies born to teens are born to single parents.

- Three quarters of the young men who become fathers drop out of school to seek employment.

Of course, it has never been the case that all youths have completed all of these steps and completed them in the prescribed order — there always have been and always will be hasty school exits, job searches, and marriages as a result of unintended pregnancies. But never before have the consequences been as severe.

Pregnant girls and teen parents, both males and females, leave school now as they always did. But today, when they drop out of school, these teens are left behind by their peers who not only go on to complete high school but to enter college as well. They are no longer just one or two years short of the average schooling attained by their peers, but four or more. And in today's labor market, those lost years are costly. So while teen parents have perhaps always been at a disadvantage relative to their peers who delayed childbearing, they are at a greater disadvantage in today's labor market than they have ever been before and, consequently, are at greater risk of being poor.

- In 1984, 65 percent of teen workers earned incomes below the poverty line for a family of three.

- Approximately one-third of the young women who give birth as single parents receive welfare.

- Three quarters of the single mothers under the age of twenty-five live on incomes below the poverty level. Young married couples are less likely to be poor, but they are still three times as likely to be poor than older couples.

Solid basic reading and math skills, a high school diploma, and delayed parenthood are rapidly becoming essential prerequisites of minimal economic survival. And increasingly, two parents, two diplomas, and two incomes are required for economic security once childbearing has begun. We need to find ways to convince all of our young people to delay parenthood, and ways to help all of them develop the skills, find the opportunities, and gain the experiences they need to be economically prepared for parenthood.

While there is still no consensus about whether society should encourage abstinence versus contraception as our primary prevention method, there can be little debate that the success of any pregnancy prevention effort ultimately lies in impressing upon teens the absolute necessity and logic of doing one of these two things. The question is, of course, how? One important answer has been that we need to provide more sexuality-specific information, guidance, and services. The greater the barriers to receiving this kind of information and the necessary services, the greater the risk of early sexual activity or pregnancy.

Research studies suggest that increasing information and services does not increase sexual activity but may increase sexual responsibility and contraceptive use among sexually active teens. The Alan Guttmacher Institute found that while American teens are about as likely to be sexually active as teens in similarly developed countries, they are twice as likely as teens in France, England, Wales and Canada, and seven times as likely as teens in the Netherlands to experience pregnancy during adolescence.

American teens need better and more timely access to the sexuality-related information, advice (including the advice to postpone sexual activity), and services that give them the capacity to delay pregnancy. But capacity is only half of the equation. In the absence of compelling reasons to avoid early parenthood, the likelihood of early sexual activity and pregnancy is high.

Research reviewed by the National Academy of Sciences in their recent report, *Risking the Future*, strongly suggests that decisions about sexual activity and contraception are tied closely to teens' aspirations, feelings of self-esteem, aspirations, and perceptions of opportunities. Teens with strong achievement orientations and with clear goals for the future are less likely to become sexually active at early ages and, more likely, if they are sexually active, to be regular and effective users of contraceptives. The Children's Defense Fund reports some analyses that show a strong, positive correlation between poor basic academic skills, limited life options and early childbearing. (Figures 1 and 2)

We need to put a pregnancy prevention system in place. This system must focus on helping young men as well as young women avoid too-early sexual activity and pregnancy. For teens for whom the basic supports are there—the educational, occupational and family experiences and expectations that give them compelling reasons to want to delay parenthood—we need to offer earlier and more comprehensive sexuality education and better access to contraceptive counseling and services for those already sexually active.

For teens for whom the basic supports are weak, however, we need to offer the sexuality-specific components while simultaneously strengthening their skills, broadening their experiences, and increasing their opportunities through education, employment exposure and experience, recreation, health care and family supports.

Adolescent Pregnancy Prevention

Parenthood by Basic Skills
Levels, 16-19 Year Old Women, 1981

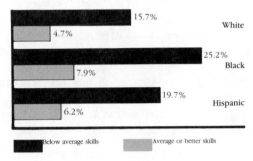

15.7%

White

4.7%

25.2%

Black

7.9%

19.7%

Hispanic

6.2%

■ Below average skills   ▨ Average or better skills

Parenthood by Poverty and Basic Skills
Levels, 16-19 Year Old   1981

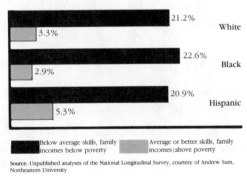

21.2%

White

3.3%

22.6%

Black

2.9%

20.9%

Hispanic

5.3%

■ Below average skills, family   ▨ Average or better skills, family
incomes below poverty   incomes│above poverty

Source: Unpublished analyses of the National Longitudinal Survey, courtesy of Andrew Sum,
Northeastern University

Reprinted with permission from the Adolescent Pregnancy Prevention Clearinghouse of
the Children's Defense Fund.

161

The urgency and the complexity of the task ahead of us is conveyed succinctly in the words of a fifteen-year-old junior high school student in Detroit who wrote that her goal is, "To go to school and fenisch my schooling whithout getting prenant."

Pregnancy prevention is the linchpin of a comprehensive set of strategies that need to be in place to prepare our youth for adulthood — strategies that address youths' need for academic education, work preparation, health services, and opportunities for personal and social development. Changes in the labor market dictate that all of our youth need the extra preparation time that delayed parenthood affords. Clear and steady evidence of progress toward adult self-sufficiency — assumed high school completion, opportunities for post-secondary education, and well-paid employment — is the grounding all youth need to maintain the motivation to delay pregnancy. Pregnancy prevention and preparation for adulthood are two sides of the same coin. The fifteen-year-old Detroit teen has two goals — pregnancy prevention and school completion — and these goals, for her and for many other teens, must be worked on together.

However, it is also necessary to expand and refine efforts to help those young men and women who are already parents. These young parents are trying to provide a decent, stable life for their children, when they themselves are too young, have low basic skills, minimal job experience, and few economic resources. Working to reduce the individual and social costs of early childbearing is essential in improving the well-being of these young families.

Issues and Analysis

Efforts to prevent adolescent pregnancy and to assist teen parents in successful parenting and self-development must be based on several themes.

First, **coordinated citywide efforts** are important. The twin challenges of preventing adolescent pregnancy and providing care for pregnant and parenting teens are extremely complex, involving the investment of a range of disciplines and agencies within a community. An important part of this effort is some coordination mechanism to ensure that resources are allocated with a minimum of fragmentation and duplication.

Second, there is the theme of **developing skills, building self-esteem, and setting priorities**. Research suggests that programs that encourage teens to stay in school, build their academic and work skills and aspirations, provide paid or volunteer work experience or expand their horizons may have an important side benefit — helping teens delay pregnancy. By helping teens develop, plan and attain their personal, social, educational and occupational goals, these programs may be teaching teens indirectly the value of delaying parenthood until progress toward meeting these goals is well underway.

Third, is the theme of **sexuality and family life education**. Because of its obvious long-term consequence — parenthood — the decision to become sexually active is perhaps one of the most important decisions an adolescent will make. Yet teens have few resources and people aiding them with this decision. Much needs to happen to ensure that adolescents have early and ample opportunities to learn and discuss this important issue and to understand its consequences. Parents need to take a more active role in initiating these discussions and in making clear their values. Schools, churches and youth-serving organizations need to become more involved. We need to build a climate in which children and teens feel comfortable seeking information, discussing concerns, and making responsible decisions about sexuality.

Comprehensive adolescent health care is the fourth theme. Against a backdrop of public opinion ranging from vehement opposition to enthusiastic support, adolescent health clinics have emerged as one viable approach to reducing pregnancies and increasing access to basic health services among teenagers. Adolescents have a wide range of health needs, including, but not limited to, sexuality and contraceptive information and services. Yet, for a variety of reasons, teenagers, especially poor teens, are less likely than any other age group to have a regular source of health care. Certainly, affordability and accessibility are barriers to care; but an equally formidable barrier is the appropriateness of that care. Adolescents are sensitive to the attitudes of health providers and are more likely to use services designed with their needs in mind, provided by caring professionals. This suggests that both basic and reproductive health care for teens ideally should be provided through comprehensive health services tailored especially for them.

Fifth, **pregnant and parenting teens are vulnerable** in a variety of ways. They, and ultimately the larger society, suffer the adverse consequences of adolescent childbearing in four main areas: health, education, employment, and economic well-being. The multiple areas of vulnerability indicate the amount of support these young households need if they are to reach, and maintain, healthy self-sufficiency. What further complicates the situation is that many of the teen parents represent low-income, sometimes minority families, who, even before giving birth, are already at risk of not being able to obtain adequate education and employment.

Profiles

There are many examples of innovative and effective pregnancy prevention programs and projects now operating. The programs presented here have been chosen to represent a broad spectrum of cities of different sizes, with different populations, and in different regions. They give a glimpse of the wide array of strategies that have been developed to address this problem both for at-risk teens and for teens who are already pregnant or parents, and an idea of the many ways cities can be involved in increasing the number and quality of efforts aimed at helping young people delay pregnancy as they prepare for adulthood.

New York City and Hartford, Connecticut, are two of the best examples of high-level citywide involvement and support. Both of these are large urban communities, serve racially-mixed populations, and have significant city involvement. Yet, despite these similarities, there are many differences, including the initiation of their activities.

Developing skills, building self-esteem, and setting priorities are at the heart of the Cities in Schools project in Atlanta, Georgia, which focuses largely on drop-out prevention; Aunt Martha's in Park Forest, Illinois which focuses on youth empowerment in a suburban area; and Wethersfield, Connecticut's Rite of Passage Experience, which aims to assist in the transition to adulthood.

The family life education program in Alexandria, Virginia is highlighted because it involves parents and the community in curriculum development and because it emphasizes training for the teachers who teach any grade of the K-12 curriculum.

Comprehensive adolescent health care is an integral part of the many components of Teen Link in Durham, North Carolina.

The Family Learning Center in Leslie, Michigan shows how to address the various difficulties that pregnant and parenting teens face through comprehensive program design and coordination of available services.

Concluding Remarks

Pregnancy prevention is critical to healthy youth development. Specific pregnancy prevention efforts can and should be incorporated into the many after-school, recreation, employment, community service and social development programs found in any community. It is likely that ten programs devoting one-tenth of their resources to dealing with sexuality-specific issues are as effective as, if not more effective than, developing one program that does that exclusively. It is also likely that this broader approach will reach more youths; engage more institutions, organizations, and citizens; and create more of a shared sense of responsibility and action on behalf of young people.

It is clear that teen pregnancy prevention is not something that can be accomplished solely through local actions. The educational and labor market changes that have heightened the negative consequences of early parenthood will require national attention. It is also clear that local efforts can progress with minimum city government involvement. But city officials and city agencies can do much to make things happen:

- coordinate public and private efforts;

- encourage agency cooperation among local groups attempting to get programs started;

- build consensus by using the powers of city hall to convene meetings and set both a tone and a direction for change; and

- commit city facilities, personnel, and resources to help solve the problems of early parenthood.

All of these are things that cities can do — and that many cities are doing.

A list of references and resources follows the profiles on page 192.

Program Location	Population, Year Geography Initiated		Budget	Municipal Involvement	Client Population	Services Provided	Outcome Data	Comments
New York, NY	Urban northeast 7,071,030	1984	$160,000	City initiated city-wide coordination	City-wide comprehensive	None		Coordination with all city agencies; 3 full-time staff
Hartford Action Plan Hartford, CT	northeast 136,392	1985	$1.01 million Public/private	Mayoral endorsement	5,000 youths and parents re prevention 400 women re maternal outreach	City-wide Health	Evaluation Data	Privately initiated then city joined; 220 women at high risk of low-birth-weight babies; 480 classrooms assisted with prevention curriculum
Exodus Inc. Atlanta, GA	urban south 425,022	1971	$1.4 million Cooperation public/private		600 at-risk students	Multi-service drop out	Evaluation data	Many national sites
Aunt Martha's Park Forest, IL	Suburban midwest 26,222	1972	Public/private		4,500	Multi-service	None	34 programs and 7 sites
ROPE Wethersfield, CT	Small northeast 26,000	1981	$50 per participant	City and state funding	200 students	Sexuality education; decision making	3-year study, Yale	State model
Family Life Curriculum Alexandria, VA	Suburban south 103,217	1980		School community	School children	Sexuality education; Teacher training	Survey	Only one in state; teacher training
TeenLink Durham, NC	South 100,538	1985	$250,000	Housing authority and schools	County teenagers	Compre-hensive health	None	Church program 8 area churches
Family Learning Center Leslie, MI	Small rural midwest *	1975	$180,000	School money; local in-kind		Pregnant and parenting services	Evaluation data	State model

* population of entire Ingham County is 272,000

Programs Dealing with Adolescent Pregnancy

Adolescent Pregnancy and Parenting Services
New York, New York

Citywide coordination through mayor's office.

Contact:
Alice Radosh, Coordinator
Adolescent Pregnancy and Parenting Services
Office of the Mayor
250 Broadway
Room 1412
New York, NY 10007
212/ 566-3450

New York City's Office on Adolescent Pregnancy and Parenting Services (OAPPS) is a comprehensive citywide effort to address adolescent pregnancy. In 1984, New York established OAPPS to develop policies and programs and to coordinate and monitor adolescent pregnancy initiatives of city agencies. As a first step, OAPPS convened an Interagency Council on Adolescent Pregnancy to determine what the policies and programs should be and to plan a cohesive citywide strategy for implementing them.

The collaborative effort of the twenty city agencies comprising the Council resulted in a strategy document that outlines specific recommendations for action. Being attached to the Mayor's Office has given the Council's recommendations high priority and great visibility. The Council has not just examined the problems and recommended some solutions; it has laid out implementation plans and continues to meet regularly concerning them. According to the coordinator of OAPPS, Alice Radosh, who also chairs the Council, "If you're located directly within city government, you don't go home after the report is written...you're still around..." to deal with the realities.

The Council's plan gives priority to programs for adolescents seventeen years old and under and to programs for teens living in poverty. The strategy emphasizes efforts to reduce the incidence of first pregnancies, early and continuing services to help teen parents become independent adults and enhance their children's growth and development, and special efforts to prevent repeat pregnancies and births to teens.

New York City is home to more than one million youths between ten and nineteen, one-fourth of whom live in families with incomes below the federal poverty line. In 1984, the city's highest teen birth rates were in the ten health districts located in designated poverty areas. Overall, teens account for twelve percent of all births in New York City, and, in some districts, the figure rises to more than 20 percent. The Council's report states that approximately 28,000 mothers in New York City are still in their teens. It goes on to say that if current trends continue without additional pregnancy prevention efforts, one out of four girls aged fourteen today will become pregnant before turning eighteen, and nearly one out of eleven will give birth.

The list of specific recommendations of what must be done holds no surprises. In fact, the city is already funding or operating programs and services at some level in each of the four areas identified. The plan stipulates that family living/sex education be provided in schools at all grade levels.

A second objective calls for an extensive and sustained media campaign. The city is currently moving forward with a citywide poster campaign and has developed public service announcements for television and radio. Information and referral services are also in place; the Teen Pregnancy Networks operating in each borough of the city function as centers for information and referral for teens and for community-based agencies that serve them.

Improved access to reproductive care was stressed in the plan. The city has a direct relationship with many of the 100 public and voluntary clinics that offer reproductive health care to teens and may be able to influence broad policies and practices governing confidentiality, costs, hours, staff, etc. Also important is the development of a variety of models of comprehensive preventive health programs serving teens and offering reproductive services. There are currently thirteen school-based health clinics in the city and a multitude of community-based multi-service youth programs offering reproductive services.

Finally, the plan calls for public efforts to give youths with the greatest risk of teen pregnancy and parenthood extra help finishing school and locating job training and employment opportunities, housing, child care, parenting education, and health and mental health services. The city is already extensively involved in this area across most agencies. The Board of Education's High School Division maintains six schools for pregnant teens and provides infant/toddler child care and parenting programs in thirteen high schools, alternative schools and GED programs. The child care program is a collaboration between the Board of Education's LYFE program (Living for the Young Family through Education) and the Human Resources Administration's WIN program (Work Incentive). In addition to these programs and the on-site health care (funded by the State Department of Health), the Board of Education sponsors the TOPP program (Teen Outreach to Prevent Pregnancy) and a new school dropout prevention initiative.

A therapeutic nursery for children of Hispanic adolescents helps mothers complete their schooling and assesses and monitors the children's development. The Department of Mental Health's Mental Retardation and Alcoholism Services contracts with outside agencies to provide these services. The Department also funds a group program for young girls that focuses on issues of sexuality and an early intervention program for ten- to sixteen-year-old mothers whose children are slow to develop.

The Human Resources Administration (HRA) provides funding for Family Redirection, a comprehensive service program for teen parents, administered by the New York Urban League. HRA also funds the Young Father Project, operated by the YWCA and Vocational Foundation, Inc., which offers vocational/employment training and parent responsibility counseling for eighteen- to twenty-five-year-old fathers on relief who are not currently supporting their children. Employment training and job placement is available for teen mothers through the Department of Employment and the Youth Bureau.

The plan lays out implementation strategies for city agencies that focus primarily on how these agencies and the city's public leadership can contribute to implementing the recommendations, and calls for the participation of the private sector as well to insure the plan's success. Specifically, the Council proposes that OAPPS, in collaboration with Council members, see that the following tasks are initiated, under appropriate auspices.

- Establishment of a common set of policies among relevant city agencies and offices.

- Development of community-by-community needs assessments and local, coordinated plans. (New money, in the form of $338,000 in tax levy funds, has already been authorized to implement the needs assessment in two communities.)

- Assertion of visible city leadership on this issue. (Mayor Koch is foremost among the plan's supporters. In March, he issued a letter to city agencies urging them to cooperate with OAPPS in implementing the recommendations.)

- Initiation or expansion of core programs to combat teen pregnancy. (Approximately $670,000 has already been authorized for teacher training in family life/sex education. Additionally, school-based clinics have been expanded, and plans to include social workers and Medicaid workers in the clinics are under discussion.)

When the Mayor's Office of Management and Budget, which was represented on the Interagency Council, reviews requests for teen pregnancy-related programs, it takes into consideration the Council's priorities and implementation strategy.

To facilitate the involvement of community organizations serving teens in the city, OAPPS has published *Teen Pregnancy and Parenting Services: A Guide to New York City Municipal Agencies*, which explains the requirements, regulations, eligibility and referral procedures for city-sponsored teen pregnancy programs. (Copies of the *Guide to Municipal Agencies* and the Council report are available from OAPPS.)

The Council will continue to produce supplementary materials and develop an annual plan for coordinated interventions. Future plans will be based on the results of the community needs assessments, the evaluation of individual agency policy reviews, and the status of pivotal citywide programs.

The Hartford Action Plan on Infant Health, Inc. Hartford, Connecticut

Comprehensive planning to prevent teen pregnancy and reduce infant mortality.

Contact:
Parisky & Daniels
Hartford Action Plan Management
(Flora Parisky or Jeffrey Daniels)
140 Huyshope Avenue
Hartford, CT 06106
203/ 249-6220

In Hartford, Connecticut, preventing teen pregnancy and reducing infant mortality are considered critical parts of the city's overall economic development plan. Connecticut is the second wealthiest state in America, yet in 1980, Hartford was the nation's fourth poorest city. That same year, Hartford had the highest rate of teen pregnancy in Connecticut, the highest infant mortality rate, the highest rate of premature births, poor access to maternity services and a concentration of the most serious maternal and child health problems in seven neighborhoods in the city.

These facts led Astrida Olds, a public affairs officer with Connecticut Mutual Life Insurance Company, to convene a series of 7:30 a.m. meetings with city officials, public health professionals, and banking industry representatives to find out how they could save newborn lives. Known locally as "The Blueberry Muffin Club", this group assessed the status of local efforts to address these problems and made recommendations for private sector involvement. The result of these sunrise symposiums was the five-year Hartford Action Plan on Infant Health.

The plan concentrates on seven Hartford neighborhoods with high rates of infant mortality and places special emphasis on reaching pregnant women and adolescents from black and Hispanic families. The plan went into effect in 1985, with a first-year operating budget exceeding $425,000 ($178,000 in public money), and began to coordinate and provide funds for initiating projects, connecting programs and enhancing existing activities. In Olds' view, "We took a haphazard array of well-intentioned groups and wove them into a whole, much like a quilt." The Hartford Action Plan on Infant Health, Inc. is managed by Parisky & Daniels, a public policy and management consulting firm. The public health projects of the plan are directed by the Hartford Department of Health.

The Action Plan has two major goals: to create a permanent capacity among community leaders and organizations to wage an aggressive, long-term, community education effort on adolescent health and infant mortality issues, and to improve the outcome of pregnancy by enhancing access and use of prenatal services for residents of the target neighborhoods. Policy direction and governance is provided by a high-level, thirteen member Board of Directors. Four committees coordinate the work toward the plan's goals: the Operating Committee oversees program development and operations, and the Maternal Health Committee, Community Mobilization Committee, and Preterm Birth Committee are each responsible for special projects focused on a specific approach to the problem for varying populations.

The Maternal Health Committee's Maternity and Infant Outreach Project (MIOP) is a comprehensive effort to improve methods to locate pregnant women and get them into care early. This effort uses aggressive outreach, referral, and follow-up and coordinates a team of neighborhood health workers and other support staff to reach into the community.

The Community Mobilization Committee oversees two initiatives. The Church/Civic Mobilization Project is a large-scale campaign to mobilize the city's churches, schools, civic and youth groups to prevent adolescent pregnancy. Youth and their parents are reached with specially-designed programs that expand critical thinking and help participants negotiate the system and increase their self-esteem and decision-making abilities. The project has established several school-related programs including a career fair which reaches 3,000 annually. The project has also developed a model program for boys, called "Always on Saturday." The program, focused on boys between the ages of nine and thirteen, meets weekly to discuss sexual issues, learn about job opportunities, take field trips, and discuss responsibility and decision-making. This program has already been replicated by the local Urban League.

The second initiative, the School-Based Health Education Project, is a joint project of the Hartford Public Schools and the Action Plan. The project seeks to expand family life education for Hartford youths by helping the schools provide health education to their students at all grade levels.

Adolescent Pregnancy Prevention

The Preterm Birth Committee oversees the Preterm Birth Prevention Project in six hospitals and community health centers. This project, begun late in 1986, has three major elements: a coordinated service intervention model; a uniform, citywide, risk assessment tool; and implementation of improved access to specialized health care for residents of the seven target neighborhoods, and by 1988, for all residents of the city.

Staffing for the Action Plan varies by project. MIOP has a staff of eleven: a director, three community health educators, one citywide outreach worker, and six community outreach workers. The Community Mobilization Project has a youth/parent program director, a part-time administrative assistant, and a health resource teacher; it contracts with a pool of facilitators to implement individual programs. The Preterm Birth Prevention Project has a nurse coordinator and three preterm risk instructors.

The major accomplishments of the Action Plan's projects are impressive. Recent highlights include:

- School-Based Health Education Project

    - The Action Plan/School Health Curricula and supporting projects were adopted for citywide use in all schools.

    - The Project conducted 320 master lessons and more than 100 conferences to train pre-kindergarten through sixth-grade teachers in family life education.

    - Educational packets were developed, and 800 students and teachers were reached through the Healthy Me project.

    - A citywide teacher in-service training program on human sexuality was attended by more than 500 teachers.

- Church/Civic Mobilization Project

    - More than 4,000 youths and their parents -nearly three times the 1986 number -were directly involved in church/community-related programs.

    - A major joint activity with Weaver High School reached all juniors and seniors and involved school staff in a three-day program on the importance of preventing adolescent pregnancy.

- A major initiative, A Celebration of Dreams, planned and developed in cooperation with the Hartford Public Schools reached 3,000 eighth graders with career education.

- Preterm Birth Prevention Project

  - The project has implemented prenatal clinical services at six locations. More than eighty women identified as at risk for preterm birth are seen weekly or bi-weekly by a preterm prevention nurse.

  - An extensive, citywide educational effort concerning preterm birth prevention measures was conducted in thirty sessions for 234 health care workers representing the six Hartford prenatal clinics, all hospital maternity units, all city emergency rooms, and health agency staffs.

- Maternity and Infant Outreach Project

  - First trimester registration for prenatal care in the target neighborhoods (a key precursor to improved pregnancy outcome) reached 53.4 percent, a 10 percent increase over the 1985 figure.

  - The low-birth-weight rate among MIOP babies was 5.9 percent, compared to a 12.7 percent rate for other city programs, representing a continuing trend in reduction of low-birth-weight infants.

In 1985, the Action Plan hired the Urban Institute of Washington, D.C. to conduct an independent evaluation of the program. In its 1986 report, the Institute stated: "Unlike more limited demonstration projects addressing these problems in other parts of the country, the Hartford Action Plan has developed a large scale strategy designed to create permanent change in the way the Hartford service delivery system, both formal and informal, responds to these problems."

Despite the plan's successes, it still faces some limitations. First, it cannot yet measure trends in teenage pregnancy rates by neighborhood, and it has been equally hard to accurately measure reductions in infant mortality rates in the short term. Second, according to Carolyn Delgado, the director of Youth/Parent Programs, they have not been very successful in reaching "hard-core youth" — those who are not involved in community activities, do not attend church and are not enrolled in school. Plans are now being made to coordinate the efforts of the project with local employment and training agencies, where these youth may be more likely to surface.

The 1987 budget for the plan is $1.01 million, with public sector contributions totaling $330,000. The Action Plan has assembled a Board of Directors of high-powered Hartford citizens that has included, from its outset, key city leadership, including former mayor Thirman Milner and former deputy mayors Alphonse Moratta and Rudy Arnold. In 1987, Congresswoman Barbara Kennelly joined the Board.

Within the city, the Hartford Action Plan has become a model for addressing other human service and education issues. The extent to which the plan is transferable to the issues of other jurisdictions has been questioned many times. The substantial amounts of corporate dollars available in Hartford rarely exist in other cities. Maxine R. Dean, who chairs the plan's Operating Committee, notes that "...we have been blessed and fortunate to have money...but there has always been money in Hartford. Other efforts in the city have had lots of money, too, but have not been successful. Money is not the crucial issue here...it's the commitment and the work of people that has made the Hartford Action Plan a success."

She believes that the Hartford Action Plan can, indeed, be replicated in other cities. "If you have a New York City or a Washington, D.C., the plan can be replicated on a smaller scale — by neighborhood, by community or by district."

What is likely to happen in Hartford in the post-Action Plan years of the next decade? The people involved in the plan hope that local agencies will institutionalize its efforts to reduce teen pregnancy with continued public and private sector support; that the outreach program for pregnant women will be stabilized over time as its most successful activities are incorporated in city- and state-funded programs; and that other cities will replicate the program.

In the short space of two-and-a-half years, Hartford has created a replicable and unique model to deal effectively with infant mortality and adolescent pregnancy, their symptoms, and their causes. One key to its success is an organizational strategy that includes a public/private partnership among city government, corporations, and foundations. The Hartford Action Plan deserves praise as an example of a cooperative, broad-based, powerful force that internalized local concerns, verbalized community needs, mobilized public and private actors, and formalized a plan to connect multi-year funds in a long-term effort to meet a serious community need.

Exodus, Inc.
Atlanta, Georgia

Providing life choices through dropout prevention.

Contact:
Neil Shorthouse, Executive Director
Exodus Cities in Schools
1011 West Peachtree Street
Atlanta, GA 30309
404/ 873-3979

Exodus, Inc., opened its doors at Atlanta's West End Academy (also known as Academy T) in 1971, with the goals of reducing the number of dropouts in the city and offering troubled teenagers opportunities for success. Building self-esteem and developing a realistically positive view of one's future—these are cornerstones of successful teen pregnancy prevention. In 1974, Exodus, a private, nonprofit organization, joined with the Atlanta Public School System to operate a Cities in Schools (CIS) program—a national model for communities seeking solutions to the growing numbers of students not completing high school.

More programs opened at St. Luke's Academy and Southside High School in late 1974, at Rich's Academy in 1982, and, most recently, at North Avenue Academy in 1987. Each of the five Atlanta CIS sites integrates education and social services based on partnerships between the public and private sectors, use of schools or alternative education sites, and reassigning staff from other agencies.

Cities in Schools is a national, nonprofit corporation dedicated to coordinating and delivering human services to at-risk youth and their families. The CIS concept evolved from the Street Academy, a New York City program that operated outside of or parallel to the schools. In 1970, the Street Academy concept evolved into the Cities in Schools program, which focuses on bringing the resources of the cities into the schools.

Through 1981, the Atlanta-based CIS programs received substantial support from the federal government. Over the years, Exodus has broadened the sponsorship of the program so that CIS now has many agencies, companies and individuals sharing in the financing and day-to-day operation of the programs.

- Exodus, Inc. provides overall administrative, fund-raising, and evaluation services for all five sites;

- Atlanta Public Schools provides teachers and supplies;

- City of Atlanta supplies social service staff, facility rehabilitation and money through Community Development Block Grants;

- Fulton County provides grants for administrative support and assigns workers from the Health Department, Food Stamp Agency and the Department of Family and Children's Services;

- Rich's Department Store provides space in its store and volunteer help;

- Metropolitan Atlanta Boys' Clubs assigns full-time staff to involve CIS youth in a range of activities;

- Neighborhood Justice Center trains CIS staff and students in conflict resolution;

- St. Luke's and All Saints Episcopal Churches provide space and offer financial and volunteer support from their congregations;

- Junior League of Atlanta funds a computer learning lab and provides volunteer staffing.

Additional support is donated by other local organizations and individuals.

The operating budget for the 1987-88 school year is approximately $1.7 million. That figure includes $841,250 from the local school system, $123,500 in contracts from the City of Atlanta and Fulton County, $563,000 in private cash donations, and $200,960 from private agencies and organizations.

Most students entering the Exodus program have either dropped out of school or have a history of truancy problems. Each CIS site enrolls approximately 100 students who enter the program through a referral and case management system. In 1987, approximately eight students were refused entry each week because of overcrowding.

Possibly the most widely heralded of the five Atlanta programs is Rich's Academy. Located inside Rich's Department Store in a 6,000 square foot space, the program began as a school of last resort for 110 students who were failing and dropping out of traditional high school programs.

In addition to providing the space for the school, Rich's Department Store offers part-time employment to some students. Rich's employees volunteer their time to help students solve social, financial, legal or emotional problems that may be preventing them from attending school regularly and giving their full attention to their academic work. Teachers and supplies are provided by the public schools. Public and private organizations and individuals offer a variety of extracurricular activities, including on-the-job training, tutoring assistance, and a "Partners" counseling program. The City of Atlanta, Fulton County, ACTION and other community service agencies provide students with access to financial, legal, health, drug and employment-related services and counseling. Because the program offers services the student may need all under one roof, time away from school is minimized.

Rich's Academy has received national attention not only because of what it does, but because of where it does it — within a department store. The Rich's model is currently being replicated in Houston by Foley's Department Store and will soon be replicated by a major department store merchant in Cincinnati, Ohio.

The Exodus Cities in Schools program has demonstrated the unique viability of citywide systems that rely, not on new outlays of money to underwrite programs, but on a more cost-efficient use of all existing resources aimed at the at-risk population. The successes of the five-site program are overwhelming. As a result of the CIS intensive support system, students who had been on the verge of dropping out are doing things they had not imagined possible: graduating, finding jobs or going on to college. Of the 592 students registered for the programs in 1986-87, 66 received high school diplomas, 209 returned to CIS for the 1987-88 school year, 103 returned to an Atlanta Public School or entered another special program, and 39 obtained employment and left school.

A study of the fiscal impact of the CIS programs during 1986-87 reported that "CIS generates a return of from $7 to $9 million in increased tax revenues and decreased costs of welfare and incarceration for every $1.2 million invested yearly..."

The success of Atlanta's Cities in Schools program has not gone unnoticed by city officials. As Mayor Andrew Young once put it, "Cities in Schools makes sense to me because it views the education of all of our young people as a responsibility all of us must share in if we are to be successful."

For further information on the various other sites of Cities in Schools projects, contact Margaret Nieto, Communications Manager, Cities in Schools, 1023 15th Street NW, Washington, D.C. 20005; 202/861-0230.

Aunt Martha's
Park Forest, Illinois

Pregnancy prevention through youth empowerment.

Contact:
Nina Albrecht
Aunt Martha's Youth Service Center, Inc.
224 Blackhawk
Park Forest, IL 60466
312/ 747-2701

By emphasizing youth empowerment, Aunt Martha's, a community-based youth center in Park Forest, Illinois, tries to give young people the opportunity to practice management skills, increase their self-esteem, and develop leadership abilities. The youths' positive feeling about their role in what they are currently doing at the Center and their influence on future activities helps build positive approaches to their own futures, including the prevention of early pregnancy.

Aunt Martha's offers comprehensive programs to help and support adolescents and their families. It was established in 1972 in Park Forest, Illinois as a result of the Youth Commission set up to give the area's adolescents a support system outside of the home. The Youth Commission, composed of young people and adults, chose the name "Aunt Martha's" to symbolize the idea of a caring individual in whom a young person could confide. Original funding for this volunteer effort came from the Village of Park Forest.

Today Aunt Martha's serves more than 4,500 adolescents and their families each year. Their small volunteer staff has grown to approximately 60 full-time staff members, 60 part-time and contractual employees, and 235 community volunteers. The program has grown from a simple drop-in counseling center to a complex array of services and opportunities.

Aunt Martha's has developed special programming and policies designed to empower youth. Its twenty-one member board of directors includes nine seats reserved for youths, and a number of young people fill both voluntary and paid staff positions at the Center. Most of the programs offered at Aunt Martha's provide growth opportunities for the participants.

Aunt Martha's serves twenty-nine communities in Southeastern Cook and eastern Will counties. It offers thirty-four programs at seven sites. Services include 24-hour crisis response, family and individual counseling, family planning clinic for teens, programs for pregnant teens, drug counseling, assistance to runaways and their families, a group home for girls, shelter for homeless youth, employment services, GED classes, tutoring, health services, temporary and long-term foster care, teen parenting assistance, legal services and crisis and delinquency counseling.

There are several levels of youth participation at the Center. Young people write, produce, and perform skits about teen sexuality and youth responsibility for adult and peer audiences. High school students in the advocacy unit are trained and employed to work with junior high students in a program called Students Involved in Pregnancy Prevention (SIPP) and teach them decision-making skills and methods for coping with peer pressure.

Funding for the program comes from private individuals, churches, service clubs, foundations, state and federal contracts, local communities, and the United Way.

The Rite of Passage Experience*
Wethersfield, Connecticut

Developing self-esteem and resisting peer pressure to prevent pregnancy and to grow toward adulthood.

Contact:
David Blumenkrantz, Director
ROPE
Department of Youth Services
Wethersfield, CT 06109
203/ 529-8611, ext. 300

The Rite of Passage Experience (ROPE) is a program designed to encourage
positive youth development by helping youth to increase or develop self-esteem,
self-awareness, decision-making abilities, personal power and understanding of
peer pressure. These skills in turn focus youths' attention on positive life choices
and help prevent too-early sexual activity.

ROPE, a 19-hour, six- to eight-week curriculum is taught in the sixth grade in
Wethersfield, Connecticut, a predominantly white suburban community, and has
been replicated in a racially mixed East Hartford elementary school. Designed
as a ritual of passage for young people growing toward adulthood, the program
was developed for eleven- to thirteen-year-old youths in transitional grades and
has also been used for older students. The program's founder, David
Blumenkrantz, felt that by giving kids a unique experience, it would serve as a
marking point in their transition to adulthood.

The ROPE curriculum is not limited to an in-class course. It is an experience that
gives young people the opportunity to learn decision-making, problem-solving

---

*   The Rite of Passage Experience is a copyright of David Blumenkrantz
    and Becce Reslock.
    ROPE is a trademark of the Rite of Passage Experience.

and peer pressure resistance skills and to enhance their self-concept while increasing self-awareness. The program begins with low-stress, group problem-solving exercises and ends with a final challenge — rock climbing or rappelling or some other four- to six-hour outdoor challenge. The activities are preceded and followed by a group discussion. The program draws heavily on the parents and the community to provide space for activities, as well as opportunities for those activities to take place.

The ROPE program was developed in 1981, and tested in several Wethersfield schools in the 1982-83 school year. In 1985, it was endorsed for all schools by the Wethersfield Board of Education and was placed at the sixth grade level as part of the K-12 Wellness Curriculum. Since it is part of the required school curriculum, sixth graders participate. The facilitators are required to go through a training program with Blumenkrantz and one of his colleagues. The program is funded by the town, and, at the end of the program, surveys are distributed to participants, their families and the community. These surveys have reflected positive feelings and a great deal of support for ROPE.

In East Hartford, the ROPE program is funded by a grant through the Connecticut State Office of Policy and Management. It is sponsored by the East Hartford Department of Youth Services (DYS), which, in 1985, was looking for a positive youth development project to be implemented in conjunction with the local schools. In its first year, Blumenkrantz and colleague Becce Reslock trained the school teachers as well as members of the DYS staff. The program is carried out in O'Brien Elementary School during school hours, although it is not a part of any curriculum. Participants take time from their classroom activities to participate in the program. Teachers no longer participate because it is difficult to arrange for substitutes for the hours away from the classroom. As a result, the program is now taught primarily by DYS staff, although the school principal continues to participate. Their ROPE program culminates with a rock climb; the Town Council, after learning about the program, also accomplished this final challenge.

The East Hartford ROPE program has been evaluated by Yale University. The preliminary report indicated that ROPE has some positive effects on its participants including increased involvement with their families (family involvement increased by 4 percent for participants and decreased by 7 percent for the control group), attachment to school (down only 2 percent among participants compared with 33 percent for the control group), increased prosocial values, and decreased feelings of alienation. Further studies will analyze misbehavior, delinquency, and drug and alcohol abuse and other indicators.

In 1985, the State of Connecticut selected ROPE as a model program and is currently funding its replication through the Office of Policy and Management. Thus far, almost 1,000 students have gone through the program, including special education students.

As the one replication thus far proves, ROPE does not have to be a part of the core school curricula nor does it have to be taught by teachers. Incorporation into the school's main functions does help to institutionalize the program and to ensure maximum student participation, but it is not mandatory.

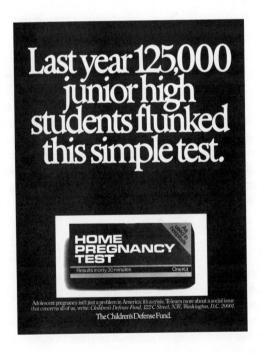

This poster is part of the Children's Defense Fund's media campaign against teen pregnancy. Used with permission.

Family Life Curriculum
Alexandria, Virginia

Teaching family life and sexuality to prevent early pregnancy.

Contact:
Jean Hunter
Alexandria Public Schools
3801 West Braddock Road
Alexandria, VA 22302
703/ 998-2160

The family life education curriculum taught from kindergarten through high school in all Alexandria public schools is one of the most extensive in the country. The program got its start in 1980 when a group of concerned parents approached the Alexandria City School System asking for a comprehensive family life curriculum for all grades. The school board immediately set up a task force to oversee the careful and complex development of a family life education program. Working with the parents and using the guidelines set forth in 1979 by the Virginia State Education Department, the Task Force and a consulting firm hired by the school board came out with curriculum recommendations in 1981. The school board approved the curriculum, and the first stage of implementation began in September 1981.

The Task Force became the Family Life Advisory Committee, which is made up of parents, residents, church, PTA, community, and health service representatives, students, and educators. Their responsibilities included making comments and recommendations and overseeing all aspects of the curriculum. Meanwhile, each of the twelve Alexandria city schools selected a parent representative, and each school, following the Advisory Committee's approval, would also review the curriculum. Finally, before the curriculum became final, meetings were held in each of the schools to allow all parents to come in and look over the proposed program.

The program has been implemented in stages. During the 1981-1982 school year, the ninth grade curriculum was tested in two classes. Alexandria began its curriculum with the ninth grade because that grade presents the complete life cycle course. Each of the grades start with two pilot programs for one school year (so any wrinkles can be ironed out before full implementation); the following year, the program is implemented completely. Each year, Alexandria implements and introduces two grade levels of the K-12 curriculum; by the 1988-1989 school year, the program should be fully implemented. At the beginning of each class, parent handbooks are sent home detailing each lesson and when it will be taught. The handbooks also include synopses of films being shown and suggested follow-up exercises that permit the parents to reinforce what the child is learning.

An important aspect of the Alexandria program is its intensive teacher training. The school system provides and pays for the graduate-level courses specifically designed for the Alexandria teachers through the University of Virginia. All teachers are invited to take the courses. The two-and-a-half-year weekly training program for secondary school teachers includes a course on the methods and materials needed to teach a course dealing with sexuality. Elementary teachers are also invited to participate in the program, although it is a little more difficult because the elementary curriculum is integrated in the existing programs. Any teacher uncomfortable with the material does not have to teach it.

Although teacher training will formally end in 1987, recurrent training and workshops will be offered. This process will cover any and all new material and will give the teachers opportunities to discuss the curriculum and materials and voice their concerns.

Although neither the teachers nor the program have been formally evaluated, curriculum specialists and department heads often observe the educators teaching the curriculum. For the ninth grade program, a survey is distributed to both the students and parents so they can evaluate the teachers and the material. The responses thus far have been very positive.

Last year Alexandria began parent-child workshops. The two series of workshops (4th-5th grades and 7th-8th grades) are designed to foster parent-child communication during five two-hour sessions. The first of these sessions is for parents only, and it sets much of the agenda for the following four sessions.

Alexandria's program is very successful because of its parental support, its conscious effort to continuously involve parents, its gradual implementation, and its intensive teacher training and support. Some opposition did arise, but it was overruled by the majority of parents actively involved in ensuring that their children would receive family life education. In 1985, the ninth grade curriculum won the "excellence in education" award at Virginia Polytechnical Institute. It is a model because, in the words of Alexandria instructor Bruce Rodenberg, "sharing responsibility with the community...is really the key to a successful program."

Teen Link
Durham, North Carolina

Comprehensive adolescent health care.

Contact:
Michele Bowen-Spencer, Coordinator
Teen Link
Lincoln Community Health Center
P.O. Box 52119
Durham, NC 27717
919/ 683-1316, ext. 257

"We grow with understanding" is the motto of Teen Link, a special component of the Adolescent Health Program at Lincoln Community Health Center in Durham, North Carolina.

The project, established in 1985, is the brain child of Mary E.L. Vernon, a local pediatrician, who began Teen Link in response to the area's high teen pregnancy rates, high school dropout rates, the small numbers of youth receiving preventive health care, and a high prevalence of depression and stress-related illnesses. Vernon says that the focus of Teen Link is "...to reach young people where they are and teach them positive behaviors so they can become healthy, self-sufficient adults."

Teen Link is open to all Durham County youths between ten and eighteen years of age. Participants may refer themselves; they are often informed of the project's many activities by youth groups, churches, the school system, health providers, parents, community agencies, or their peers. Using a holistic approach to health, the project views each teenager as a person who is part of a family, who goes to school and who lives in a community. Within this context, it comes as no surprise that Teen Link has formed alliances with a variety of local agencies to serve the many youth in need of their services. The Durham County Health Department, the City Parks and Recreation Department, Durham City and County Schools, Durham Housing Authority, Durham County Mental Health Department, the Department of Social Services, and North Carolina Central University are just a few of the agencies that cooperate with the Lincoln Community Health Center as partners in Teen Link.

Adolescent Pregnancy Prevention

According to Michele Bowen-Spencer, coordinator of Teen Link, "If you want to teach health care to youth, you have to use a lot of strategies." Teen Link's strategies include:

- Primary health care at the Lincoln Community Health Center, which offers:
    - general health care services;
    - pregnancy testing;
    - contraceptive counseling and education;
    - psychiatric evaluations;
    - nutritional counseling;
    - well-baby care;
    - sports physicals; and
    - referral services.
- Health promotion and disease prevention activities, including:
    - Psychosocial groups around issues of nutrition and fitness, family life skills, life management, risk-taking behavior, and teen parenting;
    - A peer health education program where teens are trained to serve as resources to other teens in eleven public housing projects, in churches and schools, and in the health center;
    - Community youth councils;
    - Activity focus groups that offer classes in aerobics, karate, computers, art, dance, etc.;
    - A school outreach program where on-site preventive health care services are provided, although neither medications nor prescriptions are administered on school premises;
    - A black male development program that focuses on the special needs, interests, and health and social risks among black teen males;
    - Teen health risk appraisals;
    - A church connection project where participating churches integrate their religious beliefs into a prevention program based on assistance

from trained adult and teen volunteers who keep the congregation informed about adolescent pregnancy and other teen health issues; administer health screens and health risk appraisals; and hold rap sessions.

- Community outreach and health education, including:
  - Community forums, discussions and workshops;
  - Volunteer programs; and
  - Teen Health Night Out, a social event or fun activity designed to stimulate teens' interest in health-related issues. During Teen Link's most recent night out, 700 teens registered for the program at a dance and rally held in the civic center.

Teen Link is staffed by a physician/director, coordinator, a nurse and a nurse practitioner, nutritionist, family health worker, community health facilitator, systems analyst, psychiatrist, counselor and secretary. The project also uses consultant services as necessary.

Teen Link, now beginning the third year of a four-year $1 million grant from the W.K. Kellogg Foundation, has become a household word in the greater Durham area. The project has been praised by city and county officials and has been endorsed by the city school superintendent.

The staff of Teen Link believes there is no other project like it in the country, but there is no reason why another one could not be started. A major goal of the project is to serve as a model for other communities to pattern programs for "reaching, teaching, and treating youth (R,T,Rx)." The project's components can be replicated in discrete pieces so that communities can take incremental steps toward providing comprehensive adolescent health services.

The Family Learning Center
Leslie, Michigan

Coordination of comprehensive services for parenting teens.

Contact:
Jean Ekins, Director
Family Learning Center
Leslie Public Schools
400 Kimball Street
Leslie, MI 49251
517/ 589-9102

The Family Learning Center (FLC) began in 1975 as a result of a 1974 study of the dropout problem among pregnant and parenting adolescents in the rural town of Leslie, Michigan. Sponsored by the Leslie Public Schools, FLC is a comprehensive, integrated program focusing on high school graduation, vocational preparation, child care, parenting skills, supportive involvement of the extended family, and relief from stress that may lead to abuse and neglect of the infants. The center is designed to coordinate the combination of services available from the state departments of Education, Public Health, Mental Health, Social Services and Legal Services in one, easily accessible facility. In 1980, the Michigan Department of Education chose it as a model site for comprehensive care for teen parents and their children.

FLC serves a predominantly white, lower middle class rural population, made up of teens and their families from seven rural school districts. The center is located in separate facilities adjacent to the Leslie High School, of which it is administratively a part. The services are offered not only to pregnant teens and teen mothers, but also to the fathers, grandparents, and other members of the extended family. Since many of the girls coming into the program live at home, FLC feels an intergenerational approach is critical. Family counseling, a men's group, grandparent workshops, job placement assistance, community workshops, psychology classes, home visits, a grandparents newsletter, and school credit for child development and parent training classes are some of the services offered to the extended family.

FLC also depends on the support and involvement of the community. Graduates' families are an important base of support—donating clothing, food, toys, and equipment. Volunteers from the community offer their assistance for special projects at FLC and on field trips. Michigan State University places student teachers, student nurses, and community service interns at the center for senior and post-graduate internships. Landlords keep FLC informed about rental vacancies, and employers pass on new job openings. In addition, the March of Dimes, United Fund, Cancer Society, Muscular Dystrophy Association, Heart Foundation, La Leche League, and others provide educational materials and speakers. Doctors and dentists offer free services that complement the care available in local clinics.

FLC's child care center is licensed to serve daily twenty-six children between the ages of two-and-a-half weeks and six years. It is the only infant child care center in the rural part of the county. It maintains a 1:4 staff-to-child ratio for infants, and a 1:6 staff ratio for toddlers. The center cares for children up to six years old, allowing teen parents with older children to participate in the program. The child care center operates approximately nine months out of the year, closing during the summer.

Parent training at FLC involves taking four academic courses as well as spending one hour per day during the first semester working in the child care facility. On a year-round basis, FLC offers health services for both the mother and her child, counseling, and assistance with job placement and child care arrangements.

FLC's annual operating budget is $180,000. Funds for the program come from the state departments of Education, Social Services and Public Health. The seven school districts that send students to FLC reimburse the Leslie School District for the costs of the academic component. The Leslie School District pays for classroom materials and supplies as well as the three full-time teachers in the school. FLC continues to meet with state officials to ensure that pregnant and parenting teen services remain a priority.

FLC has been evaluated along with the seven other state model programs by the High/Scope Educational Research Foundation of Ypsilanti, Michigan. The three-year evaluation testifies to the programs' success:

- In 1985, 91 percent of its pregnant and parenting seniors graduated;

- In 1985, 97 percent of its pregnant and parenting eighth to eleventh graders stayed in school;

- Over the past three years, infants born to FLC students have had a lower than average medical complication rate, higher birth weights, and fewer respiratory problems. Of sixty births, one child was born prematurely, four at low birth weight, and one with a birth defect.

- Over three years, there were only two repeat pregnancies to single teen mothers, and three to married mothers. In a recent three-year study, the national rate of repeat pregnancies was thirty-three percent; the rate at model sites in Michigan (including FLC) was 2.4 percent.

- The children of teen parents demonstrated marked improvement in their socialization, motor and verbal skills.

- Teen parents had increased grade point averages, improved attitudes and behavior, greater confidence in their abilities and higher self-esteem.

The Leslie Public School System is one of ten programs in the country that received a Ford Foundation Innovations in State & Local Government Award Program Grant. The $80,000 grant will help the Family Learning Center meet several of its current needs, including new classroom facilities, improved child care facilities, and creation of a small learning lab. It will also be used to disseminate information about the program throughout other jurisdictions and support a study of the program's long-term effects on the families it serves. A portion of the grant will provide matching support for a scholarship fund for outstanding FLC graduates who wish to pursue vocational training or academic studies at community colleges and universities.

Resources

Additional Programs

Other programs that relate to developing skills, building self-esteem, and setting priorities include:

El Puente
211 South 4th St.
Brooklyn, NY 11211
718/387-0404
Luis Garden-Acosta
Chief Executive Officer

El Centro de la Comunidad Unida
United Community Center
1028 S. 9th Street
Milwaukee, WI 53204
414/384-3100
Ricardo Diaz
Executive Director

Other programs that relate to sexuality and family life education include:

Teen Choice: Pregnancy Prevention Counseling
Inwood House
320 E. 82nd Street
New York, NY 10028
212/861-4400
Mindy Stern, Director,
Community Outreach Program

The Girls Club of Dallas
5415 Maple Street
Suite 222
Dallas, TX 75232
214/630-5213
Pat Lysell, Executive Director

Other programs that relate to comprehensive adolescent health include:

Youth Health Service, Inc.
971 Harrison Avenue
Elkins, WV 26241
304/636-9450
Frances Jackson
Executive Director

Jackson-Hinds School-Based
Adolescent Health Program
P.O. Box 3437
Jackson, MS 39207
601/362-5321
Maxine Orey
Director of Adolescent Services

West Dallas Youth Clinic
3131 Northampton
Dallas, TX 75212
214/688-3108
Truman Thomas, Director

Other coordinated citywide efforts include:

Minneapolis Adolescent Pregnancy and Parenting Project
127 City Hall
Minneapolis, MN 55415
612/348-2100
Jan Hively, Deputy to the Mayor

Adolescent Pregnancy Prevention

Publications

Risking The Future: Adolescent Sexuality, Pregnancy, and Childbearing (Vol. I & II)
National Research Council
National Academy Press
2101 Constitution Avenue, NW
Washington, D.C. 20418

Preventing Teenage Pregnancy: A Public Policy Guide
Susan E. Foster
The Council of State Policy and Planning Agencies
Hall of the States
400 North Capitol Street
Suite 291
Washington, D.C. 20001

Organizations

Adolescent Pregnancy Prevention Clearinghouse
Children's Defense Fund
(publisher of bimonthly series of reports)
122 C Street, NW
Washington, D.C. 20001
(202) 628-8787
Sharon Adams-Taylor, Coordinator

National Organization on Adolescent
Pregnancy and Parenting (NOAPP)
P. O. Box 2365
Reston, VA 22090
(703) 435-3948
Sharon Rodine, Director

Center for Population Options
1012 14th Street, NW
Suite 1200
Washington, D.C. 20005
(202) 347-5700
Judith Senderowitz, Executive Director

Subjects & Predicates

Chapter VII

Lessons Learned

by John E. Kyle

There are both moral and economic imperatives for our nation to reverse its failure of our children and youth. With more than one-in-five (21 percent) children growing up in poverty (31 percent in Boston) the moral imperative for action derives from signs of an evolving permanent underclass in America, an underclass inimical to democratic ideals and one in which children are relegated to lives of hopelessness and despair. The economic imperative, on the other hand, is driven by demographic predictions of labor shortages, and a growing mismatch of undereducated workers and jobs which require increasingly higher levels of basic skills.

Mayor Raymond Flynn, Boston

The previous five chapters describe major issues affecting children and families and present profiles of programs and policies in more than thirty cities and towns across the United States. These communities reflect many differences in size, geography and style of government. They are alike, however, in that they are heeding Mayor Flynn's imperatives: in each of them, local programs and policies are helping children and families improve their lives.

The programs profiled in this book suggest a number of specific lessons that can serve as a set of guiding principles for developing and implementing future programs and policies.

A first lesson is the realization that **leadership is crucial.** One person can begin a project. Many of the efforts among these profiles were created through such leadership. The profiles show mayors in Seattle, Dallas, Minneapolis, and elsewhere who used administrative or political clout; a foundation in Pittsburgh that used financial persuasion; citizen advocates in Durham and Alexandria who used organizing ability; and a civic leader in Hartford who used the strength of humanitarianism. Any leader can use the model described by Indianapolis Mayor William Hudnut III: "My role as mayor is three jobs: a coach who develops strategy, a player in the game, and a cheerleader." In order to get an issue or problem addressed, a mayor or foundation official can use the power or prestige of office to call people together informally or to convene a task force or blue ribbon panel. Advocates and humanitarians can call upon their passion and the strength of their convictions to gather support for new ideas and projects. It is important to identify and encourage such leadership.

A second lesson learned from the profiles is that **vital and reliable facts about a problem are needed to help in establishing effective leadership.** In *Families in Peril*, Marian Wright Edelman points out that "...thorough homework—good fact-finding coupled with good analysis—is essential....misleading facts can discredit a leader and a cause." The profiles show that surveys to collect data and citizen views have been used successfully in Seattle, Toledo, Sacramento, and elsewhere. A strategic planning guide for analyzing a city's services was recently published by the Annie E. Casey Foundation for cities competing in its New Futures project. In its January 1987 Adolescent Pregnancy Prevention Clearinghouse report, the Children's Defense Fund provided a series of checklists to determine how local institutions and professions are addressing critical issues affecting a community's children and families. Although the checklists are specific to teen pregnancy, they can be readily adapted to other issues. Effective fact finding can lead to effective problem-solving.

A third lesson is that **public-private partnerships or collaborations can strengthen the efforts of everyone involved.** In many of these profiles, success comes because of the involvement of both the public sector and the private sector, including funders, corporations and private citizens. Consider again the notion of government support and charitable foundation support complementing each other, as they do in Pittsburgh. A city is very likely to provide some core services to children and families (e.g. many of those provided through a local health department). But city officials are unlikely or unwilling to risk public monies to fund pilot programs or innovations or to do planning or evaluation. These items, however, are what some foundations seek to fund. Foundations prefer not to fund direct services, especially core services that somebody else has a responsibility to fund, but they do like to fund new or innovative techniques, evaluation, and planning. The corporate sector, too, is interested in being supportive when their actions might complement their corporate purposes. An example is our Houston profile describing the 'adopt-a-school' activities of Tenneco, Inc. It makes good sense, then, to encourage a public/private partnership that might provide the advantages from both partners and, in so doing, facilitate sound program implementation.

Fourth, **it is important to institutionalize the effort.** If a project is worthwhile, it is important for it to continue as long as it is needed rather than only for the duration of a particular policymaker's term in office or for the duration of a particular fiery campaign of need. But how do you institutionalize personal power or passion? Continuation of the program or policy can occur formally or informally and achieving it either way is a step forward.

Informal institutionalization means that there is a sense of history about a project or effort. People know that it has been around and know about its positive effects; therefore, they want it to continue. Informal networking among organizations that are working on similar issues may not be able to make sure that the needs of children and youth are appropriately addressed every time, but at least it means that there is a history of doing things on behalf of children that can be handed down from one person to another, from one agency to another. There may not be an official process by which the project continues, but there is a commonly held sense of its staying power. Continuation no longer depends solely on that one leader who may have pulled the thing together initially. An example of informal institutionalization is the success of KidsPlace:St.Louis which has become a focal point, or "mouthpiece," for children and youth, in the words of the executive director. Although it does not yet have a permanent niche of its own, the people in St. Louis who need to know about children and youth know that KidsPlace:St.Louis is the place to go. Furthermore, such informal institutionalization can lead to more formal arrangements later.

Formal institutionalization means passing ordinances or making additions to the zoning review process or changing the regulatory or planning process in order to trigger automatic attention to the needs of children and families. San Francisco and Sacramento are among the several cities that have passed zoning and/or building codes that will help to create more child care facilities. Other examples include specific staff positions dedicated to work on behalf of children and families (perhaps in a planning mode) and administrative and budgetary units devoted to children and families. Some formal institutionalization may exist outside the government structure. For example, KidsPlace Seattle has recently replaced its informal link to city government with an incorporated non-profit body which will continue beyond the tenure of any one individual who helped to create it. Different approaches may work in different communities.

Another aspect of institutionalization is staffing. Consistent and competent staffing builds support. In fact, staff who don't stay around long undermine the program because clients are wary of the inconsistency.

Fifth, beyond public/private partnerships, the profiles show **the need to provide services in a coordinated fashion.** All the players involved in a particular set of issues must be aware of and participate with the others. Each of the issues that have been addressed in this book intersect with the others. There are children in child care whose parents are teenagers. Teen parents are among the youths who are unemployed. There are young poor families and poor children among the homeless. In addressing any one of these issue areas, it is necessary, as seen in the program in Leslie, Michigan, to take a comprehensive look across all of its facets. A teenage parent cannot build a successful life if the intersecting needs of employment, child care, and housing are not met. Programs that use such an intersecting approach are the ones being looked for by the foundations described in the Pittsburgh profile.

Sixth, **it is important to encourage high visibility** for the positive things that are happening on behalf of children and families. The point is not only to publicly reward those who have worked hard, but also to promote and demonstrate the involvement of all segments of the community whether they've been directly responsible for it or not. The visibility will ensure ownership and aid in institutionalizing the project. Seattle's annual KidsDay and New York's citywide poster campaign exemplify two different approaches to gaining greater public visibility. Encouraging mayoral support, such as Mayor Koch's backing of New York City's teen pregnancy prevention services, builds positive publicity for the services and creates a positive identification on the part of the mayor. The publicity also helps a community form a positive self-image.

Seventh, these profiles show **the importance of the community and/or neighborhood as a viable component of the policy making and program delivery process.** Officials at the community level can be more sensitive to the needs of citizens than officials at the state or federal level because they often have fewer people to represent and because they are often closer to them geographically. They know the needs of their communities. This knowledge has not always been well-used in policy making and policy planning efforts. This has happened partly because agency directors and citizen leaders haven't had the time to demonstrate this knowledge, but it is also because other people haven't been willing to listen to them. One local agency's opinion has been treated as just that: one agency's opinion. However, when one agency opinion is added to another and to another, it becomes more than one unique agency perspective. That single neighborhood data base, that knowledge of what a community accepts or rejects, and that knowledge of what works become key building blocks in any effort to conduct effective planning and development of policies concerning children and families. The profiles of programs in Wausau, Wisconsin, and Washington, D.C. show how community leaders can be effective in shaping policy.

Another lesson—the eighth—is the **crucial roles of the schools**. Schools and school systems appear in varying ways in many of the projects profiled in this book. The school system in Minneapolis is an integral part of the continuum of services. In Leslie, Michigan, the Family Learning Center for pregnant and parenting teens is housed at the local high school. High-quality early childhood programs, literacy training, and teen pregnancy prevention services occur in schools.

On the other hand, some projects described here are aimed squarely at meeting needs that the schools failed to meet. Exodus in Atlanta assists the schools in meeting the education and life goals of dropout-prone students. Tenneco, a large Houston corporation, provides similar support by adopting a specific school. In particular it appears that the Committee for Economic Development overstates the case only slightly when it concludes "the schools are ill-equipped to respond to the multidimensional problems of poor and minority youngsters."

Even the failures confirm the importance of the roles most often played by schools: ubiquitous institutions beyond the family that are child-centered and are devoted to development and preparation for the future.

The ninth lesson concerns **the importance of evaluation as a means of program development and accountability**. But the topic is not simple. Effective and useful evaluation of services to children and families is not often done, and when it is done, the process often includes inappropriate measures or mere rudimentary compilation of numbers served. However, Dr. Heather Weiss of Harvard University, a leading scholar in evaluation of family support and education programs, says that this kind of evaluation—basic and straightforward—may be the best for the kind of service being delivered. She believes that some new evaluation tools may be needed, that research means examination of the process of delivering the service as well as analyzing the results, and that intermediate results may be as important as end results. She says that it is not enough to know that a program worked, but what worked, when, for whom, how and why. It is also necessary to realize that the desired results or goal of the project may not be evident until long into the future (a poor child's becoming self-sufficient because of a high-quality early childhood education program will not be seen for two decades) or may not be evident at all (the child who doesn't develop learning or physical disabilities because its mother received pre-natal health care will never be detected). Evaluation of the program's value to society, as well as to the individuals involved, is also important.

The tenth lesson is that **careful consideration must be given to the policy approach that is undertaken in the child and family arena.** What is meant by children's policy vs. family policy vs. child and family policy? Is one better than another? A policy that only looks at families may overlook the needs of the children. A policy that looks only at children may overlook the needs of parents. For example, the teen pregnancy and parenting program that only focuses on the teenager could be an example of child policy. If it were a family policy, it might treat the issue from the perspective of how to support the parents of teens. A child and family policy approach, however, could look at the service needs of the parenting teen, the teen's parents and the teen's child. The Leslie, Michigan, program does exactly that.

The eleventh lesson is a different side of the child-and-family-policy-planning issue. Perhaps **all policies ought to have a component that refers to children and families.** In some cases that may be more important than having a separate children's policy. For example, requiring city planning departments to study the impact of new buildings or developments on children and families may be more important than having the city council adopt a resolution on children's policy or having the mayor create an office for children and youth.

In fact, a nationwide zoning survey of 219 communities by Marsha Ritzdorf of the University of Oregon demonstrates the validity of the department-by-department approach. She points out that most zoning ordinances define *family*, that many of them were drafted before 1950, and that fifty percent of the communities used these ordinances to investigate complaints. In many cases, the ordinances do not take into account the demographic forces (such as divorce, single parenting, longer life spans, dual-career families) that are reshaping the American family. They are, therefore, ripe for change.

The **inclusion of prevention is a vital element in the planning of services** and is the twelfth and final lesson. The U.S. House of Representatives Select Committee on Children, Youth, and Families reported on various prevention programs on August 14, 1985. These programs not only benefited children, but also were cost-effective. In January 1987, Chicago's Colman Fund cited "focus on prevention" as one of its six pivotal conclusions. "In failing to anticipate ... problems or to act swiftly when problems first arise, society is an accomplice in the lost potential ... We must begin to care in the beginning."

In a sense, the only lesson to be learned from this book is that there is much that should be done and much that can be done. The preceding chapters do not exhaust the general topic or the specific issue areas.

Furthermore, this book is about and for problem solvers—people who acknowledge problems, but instead of complaining, mobilize to do something about them. Thus, the basic "lesson" can be restated as: *all city leaders*—elected, appointed, or just in the right place at the right time—*can convene, broker, leverage, and join in partnerships to see to it that the needs of children and families are met*.

Readers will draw their own lessons and insights from the analyses and program profiles in this book. Perhaps theirs will be different from the ones offered here. Indeed, the authors and the National League of Cities hope and intend that this book will stimulate, encourage, and assist such constructive analysis by city officials and others. After all, our cities and our children are at stake.

References

Center for the Study of Social Policy. 1987. *The Annie E. Casey Foundation's New Futures Initiative: Strategic Planning Guide*. Washington, D.C..

Children's Defense Fund. 1987. *Adolescent Pregnancy: Anatomy of a Social Problem in Search of Comprehensive Solutions*. Washington, D.C..

The Colman Fund for the Well-Being of Children and Youth. 1987. *The Plan of Action for Children: Investments in the Future*. Chicago.

Committee for Economic Development. 1987. *Children in Need: Investment Strategies for the Educationally Disadvantaged*. New York and Washington, D.C.

Edelman, M.W. 1987. *Families in Peril*. Cambridge and London: Harvard University Press.

Ritzdorf, M. "Planning and the Intergenerational Community: Balancing the Needs of the Young and the Old in American Communities," *Journal of Urban Affairs*, V. 9, No. 1, 1987.

INFORMATION CENTER

THE CARNEGIE FOUNDATION
FOR THE ADVANCEMENT OF TEACHING

5 IVY LANE
PRINCETON, N.J. 08540